1930

Dunning Tariff – preferential treatment to British imports.

British dirigible R-100 arrives at St. Hubert, Quebec.

Gilbert LaBine discovers radium at Great Bear Lake.

British Empire Games are held at Hamilton. Jimmy Trifunov and Earl McCready win gold medals in wrestling.

Cairine Wilson becomes first woman appointed to Senate.

Control of natural resources returned to provinces of B.C., Alta., Sask., and Man.

WW I ace Billy Barker is killed in Ottawa plane crash.

Conservatives win federal election. R.B. Bennett prime minister.

Parliament enacts Unemployment Relief Act.

Robert Martin and Emil Kading are rescued after two months in frozen B.C. wilderness.

Contract bridge becomes the international rage.

Photo flashbulbs come into use.

First successful Canadian crossing of the North Atlantic by airplane by J.E. Boyd and H.P. Connor.

E.J. Pratt publishes *Verses of the Sea.*

1931

The Earl of Bessborough is appointed governor general.

British Parliament passes the Statute of Westminster.

Dust storms hit the Prairies.

Communist leader Tim Buck is arrested for sedition.

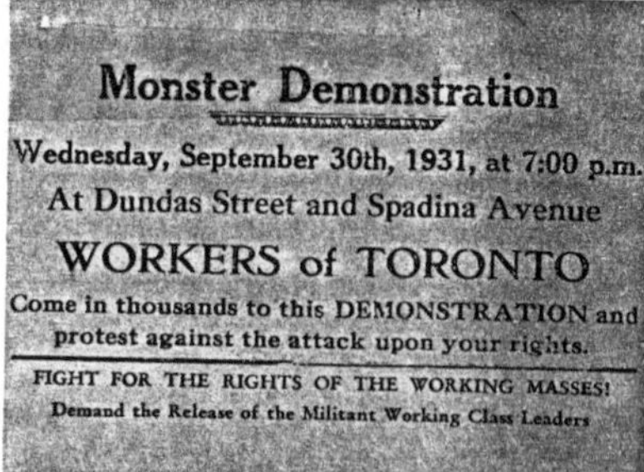

Monster Demonstration

Wednesday, September 30th, 1931, at 7:00 p.m.

At Dundas Street and Spadina Avenue

WORKERS of TORONTO

Come in thousands to this DEMONSTRATION and protest against the attack upon your rights.

FIGHT FOR THE RIGHTS OF THE WORKING MASSES!

Demand the Release of the Militant Working Class Leaders

Jackie Callura wins Canadian featherweight boxing title.

First Trans-Canada Air Pageant is staged at Hamilton, Ont.

Frank Stack of Manitoba wins U.S. speedskating championships.

Supreme Court rules radio broadcasting under federal jurisdiction.

English-born Archie Belaney publishes *The Men of the Last Frontier* under pseudonym "Grey Owl."

[illegible]nsus: 10,376,786 total p[illegible]

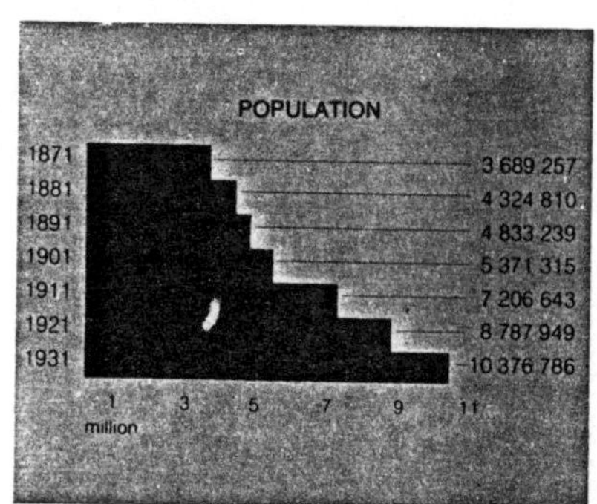

Construction of Toronto's Maple Leaf Gardens is completed.

1932

Co-operative Commonwealth Federation (CCF) is founded in Calgary.

Imperial Economic Conference is held in Ottawa.

Canadian cyclist "Torchy" Peden wins six-day race at Madison Square Garden.

"Mad Trapper" Albert Johnson is killed after 29-day manhunt.

American Amelia Earhart is first woman to fly solo across Atlantic, Nfld. to Londonderry, 13 hours 30 minutes.

Canada and U.S. sign agreement to build St. Lawrence Seaway.

Canadian champ Sandy Somervill[illegible] wins U.S. Amateur Golf title.

Dorothy Livesay publishes *Signpost.*

Federal government establishes work camps under Department of National Defence.

Dominion Drama Festival is established to promote amateur theatre groups.

New Welland Canal opens.

Parliament establishes the Canadian Radio Broadcasting Commission.

Vancouver's Duncan McNaughton and Toronto's "Lefty" Gwynne win gold medals in high jump and boxing at L.A. Olympics.

Riots erupt as 10,000 unemployed march on government buildings in St. John's, Nfld.

1933

The Group of Canadian Painters is formed from the remaining Group of Seven.

Frederick Philip Grove publishes *Fruits of the Earth.*

Unemployment hits depression high

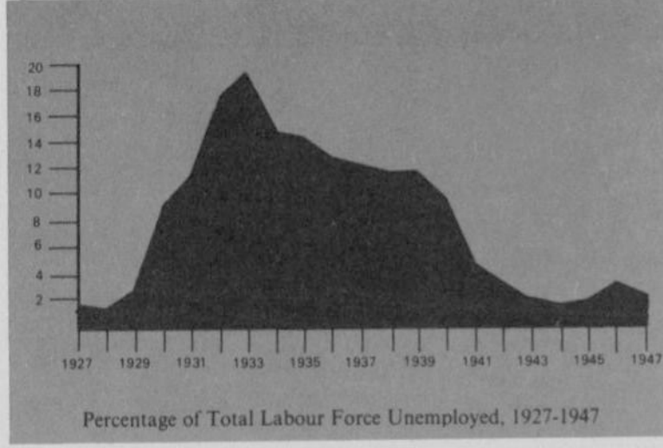

Percentage of Total Labour Force Unemployed, 1927-1947

Frank Hawks makes first non-stop flight across Canada, Vancouver to Kingston.

CCF Convention approves party platform, the "Regina Manifesto."

Regina Manifesto

(Programme of the Co-operative Commonwealth Federation, adopted at First National Convention held at Regina, Sask., July, 1933)

1934

Vancouver's Jimmy McLarnin defeats Barney Ross for the world welterweight title.

H.H. Stevens resigns from Bennett government over price spreads probe.

Morley Callaghan publishes *Such Is My Beloved.*

Canadian women, Dewar, Haslam and Pirie, take half the titles in Empire Games swimming.

Englishman Charles Bedaux leads "champagne safari" into B.C. bush.

The Bank of Canada, the nation's central bank, is created to manage monetary system.

E.J. Pratt publishes *The Titanic.*

John Labatt is kidnapped and held for $150,000 ransom.

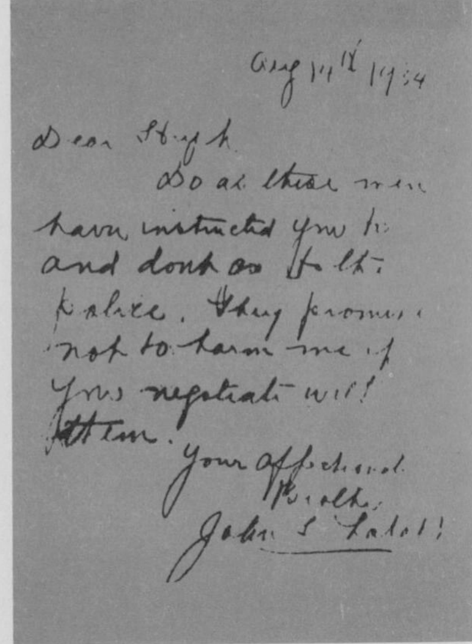

Aug 14th 1934

Dear Hugh,

Do as these men have instructed you to and don't go to the police. They promise not to harm me if your negotiations will them.

Your affectionate brother,

John S Labatt

Mitch Hepburn becomes premier of Ontario breaking almost 30 years of Conservative rule.

Newfoundland's constitution is suspended and the Island reverts to colony status.

The Dionne Quintuplets are born in Callander, Ont.

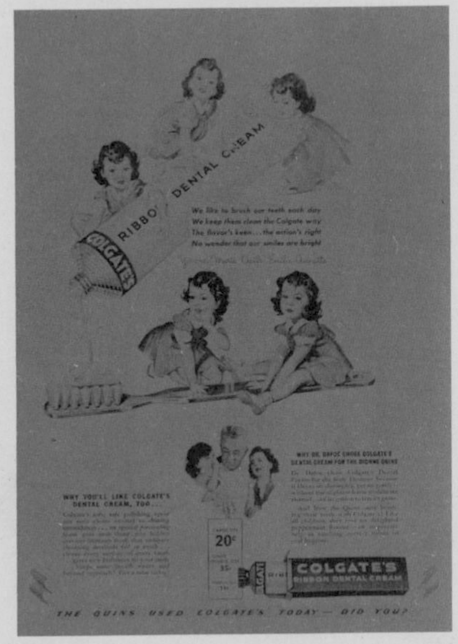

The Hungry Thirties

Thirst quenchers like these "wet the whistles" of kids and adults in the thirties, but Canada Dry was still the nation's most popular non-alcoholic beverage.

Max Braithwaite

The Hungry Thirties
1930/1940

Canada's Illustrated Heritage

Canada's Illustrated Heritage

Publisher: Jack McClelland
Editorial Consultant: Pierre Berton
Historical Consultant: Michael Bliss
Editor-in-Chief: Toivo Kiil
Associate Editors: Clare McKeon
Jean Stinson
Designer: David Shaw
Cover Artist: Alan Daniel
Picture Research: William Bilecki
Lembi Buchanan
Judy Forman
Betty Gibson
Patricia McLoughlin

ISBN: 0-9196-4425-2

N.S.L. Natural Science of Canada Limited
254 Bartley Drive
Toronto, Ontario M4A 1G4

Printed and bound in Canada

Contents

NEW YORK
ROAD SHOW
YOU CANT TAKE IT WITH YOU
GEORGE S. KAUFMAN
JUNE 8 TO 11

PROLOGUE

"You Can't Take It With You"

... if you help us out a little if we could get $10 we could probably pay you back this fall.

Letter to Prime Minister R. B. Bennett, 1935

It is New Year's Eve and a new decade is beginning. The thirties. As the New Year arrives, Canadians are jittery but hopeful. The stock market crash of October 1929 ruined a few and hurt thousands more. Construction and exports have dropped alarmingly. But most people believe the experts who predict a quick recovery. As Canadians gather at house parties across the country, the scene is much the same. There is a group around the piano, singing "I'll be down to get you in a taxi, Honey." Some are too loud, some off key, some can't manage to sing at all.

In the den a half-dozen drinkers are grouped around a new console radio ("face-to-face realism at only $251.50"), waiting for the American network broadcast of the arrival of the New Year in Times Square in New York City. It's rumoured that Amos and Andy may be on hand.

In the dining room the furniture has been pushed back and the rug rolled up for dancing to the music of twenty-seven-year-old Guy Lombardo and his Royal Canadians, from the Roosevelt Hotel in New York. Some are doing the Charleston, although this craze has passed its peak, while others are sticking to the old reliable fox trot, or flee hop. The mens' jackets have wide peaked lapels and the trousers, with many pleats in the front, come up high under the armpits. The women's skirts are below the knee and many dresses are made of cloth cut on the bias so that they cling to the figure, showing little but revealing much.

At the kitchen table four furrow-browed non-drinkers are playing that new game called contract bridge.

More serious people stand about discussing the prospects of R. B. Bennett defeating Mackenzie King in the election likely that year, or the coming visit of Jan Christian Smuts, premier of South Africa, to talk about world peace, or whether the Toronto Maple Leafs will beat the high-flying Montreal Maroons that very night.

Party or no party, ten million Canadians, old and young, were entering a decade more fantastic than they ever dreamed. Before the decade was many months old, thousands would be fired from their jobs, with no severance pay or unemployment insurance to fall back on, and they would not work again for almost ten years. Eager young people graduating that June from high schools, universities, nursing courses and teacher's colleges would not work at their professions but would pick up what they could by parking cars, driving taxis, selling encyclopedias, or subsisting in work camps.

Men who were millionaires six months before

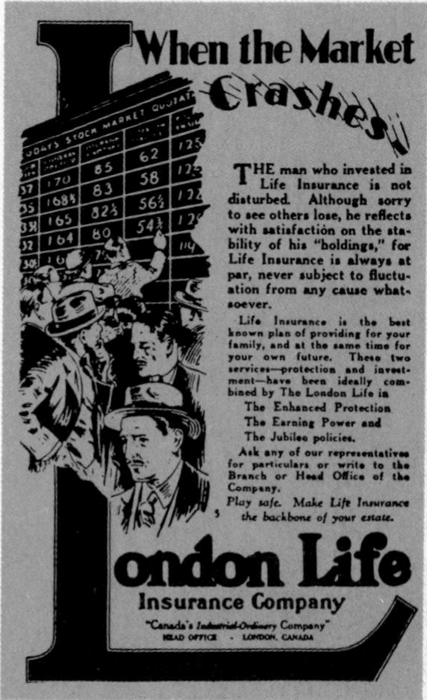

Countless Canadians who had lost their shirts in the market crash scrambled for safe investments in 1930, the date of this ad. By the height of the Depression, many questioned whether any investment could possibly be "safe."

***Opposite page:** Vancouver strikers escorted by "Scanlon's Cossacks" file past a marquee announcing the road show opening of the 1938 comic hit, "You Can't Take It With You."*

For those who could afford more than home-rolled brands, cigarettes like Spuds promised relief from the tense moments of life, real or frivolous.

or presidents of successful companies would soon be flat broke. One contractor who had had a whole street of houses under construction when the stock market crashed was so much in debt that he came home, packed everything he could into his Essex and drove away, leaving his house and furniture and business assets for his creditors to fight over.

Many men who had been too proud to ask anyone a favour would soon accept hand-me-down clothing for themselves and their families. Others would become so enraged they would march and shout and throw stones and fight the police on the streets.

Farmers who had pioneered the West would watch the topsoil of their farms blow away and the doors of the banks close against them.

To many the thirties was a decade of despair. But to many, many others – by far the majority – the thirties was a decade of adventure and change. More people would make long distance telephone calls, travel further in cars and buses, fly in style and comfort from coast to coast than ever before. Miners, trappers and traders in the north would find they were no longer isolated: the sick could be flown from Frobisher to hospital in Winnipeg, wives could be flown out for holidays, products could reach markets in days instead of months.

the chaos to come

Politically, Canada was enjoying a relatively stable period. William Lyon Mackenzie King was prime minister and had been, except for six months and eighty-nine days, since 1921. It is true that his was a minority government, but he was pretty sure of the support of the 13 Progressives in Parliament. King was absolutely unaware of the chaos to come and completely unprepared to deal with it. He would be defeated in the election of that autumn.

The leader of the opposition, soon to become prime minister, was a stern, dignified Calgary millionaire named Richard Bedford Bennett. He believed in good conservative principles, balanced budgets, strict maintenance of law and order, sound financing and the right and duty of every man to perform useful work. As with his Liberal opponent, however, there was nothing in his experience and training to prepare him for the new ideas and swift, decisive action needed to deal with the Depression. Perhaps no politician could have handled the situation better, but most Canadians were convinced after five years that few could have done worse.

the tough, prickly cactus

Thus was the stage set for the entrance of new politicians leading new parties. Like the tough, persistent prickly cactus, the new parties sprouted and grew in the fertile but dust-dry soil of the western provinces. Like the bounding Russian thistle, they thrived best in adversity and spread their seeds far and wide. Unlike the ubiquitous thistle, however, they produced fruits that were to nourish the thinking of Canadians for many years to come.

Financial conditions at the beginning of the thirties were shaky, but the mood was optimistic. Despite a small population, Canada ranked sixth among the trading nations of the world. Canadian credit on the world market was good, and the tourist trade was brisk. After decades of continued prosperity giving Canadians the second highest standard of living in the world, financial experts were agreed that the adverse conditions were temporary.

Canadian life in 1930 was prosperous, and technology was beginning to make a big difference. Houses were equipped with electricity, and labour-saving appliances were becoming common. The radio was now delivering good quality sound, filling Canadian lives with entertainment and instant information. Automobiles sold for $500 to $1,000, and the roads were dependable, even if their gravel surfaces were often as rough as washboards. The airplane was emerging as a means of moving passengers and freight, and every indication pointed to transoceanic air service for the future. There was plenty of change in the land, and it was an exciting time.

Influenced by Marlene Dietrich and other Hollywood stars, women began appearing in slacks, and smoking in public was becoming common. Men, on the other hand, were wearing short pants called plus fours for golf and casual occasions. Women were required to have short skirts on their bathing suits, while it was undesirable and in some places illegal for men to go topless.

More women were working in 1930 than ever before and the divorce rate was climbing fast. Following the lead of Agnes Macphail, a few women were elected to Parliament. In 1930 Cairine Wilson became the first woman to be appointed to the Senate.

Maclean's magazine, the leading periodical, published as many as six fiction pieces in each issue. Most were romantic stories, mysteries or adventure tales, usually set in the Canadian north or far away places. Editorials complained of the rising cost of government spending. Letters to the Editor argued either that Canada needed a new flag, or that the "good old Union Jack" should be retained. The Royal Family was scrutinized; some people felt that Canada needed no more immigrants; and many feared that Canadians were becoming too much like their American neighbours.

Influenced by Sigmund Freud and the new science of psychology, parents agonized over whether or not to spank their children. Sports fans argued over hockey violence, some saying it was getting rougher, while others claimed it was becoming much tamer. The Canadian game of rugby had changed its name to football, and the burning question here was whether or not to adopt the forward pass. Sports writer Ted Reeve argued that it would ruin the Canadian game.

Such was the Canadian mood as the thirties began. The decade known variously as "the dirty thirties," "the hungry thirties," and "the nasty thirties" changed much of that. It was a decade of technological explosion and financial disaster, a decade of instant communication, movies, airplanes, automobiles, soup kitchens, bread lines, cardboard insoles, flour-sack lingerie and penny cigarettes. During these ten years Canadians experienced conditions they would never have believed possible. And when it was over many could never shake the feeling that, regardless of how prosperous they may be, this terrible thing might happen again.

Agnes Macphail
Canada's First Woman MP

Daughter of a farm auctioneer, Agnes Macphail, born in Grey County, Ont., in 1890, was elected to the Commons in 1921. For most of the nineteen years she served in parliament, she was the only woman to hold a seat. An outspoken advocate of civil rights, social reform and health services, she was a strong supporter of the farm cooperative movement and the CCF until her retirement.

SPECIAL ATTRACTION

FREE - - FREE - - FREE - - FREE

5 Reels of Talking Pictures

(Through courtesy of Chrysler Corporation of Canada)

SEE AND HEAR MAJOR BOWES AND HIS AMATEURS ALSO

"HELL DRIVERS" "SAFETY DRIVING"

Together with a galaxy of Movie and Radio Stars in the

EMPRESS THEATRE

THURSDAY AFTERNOON, MARCH 24th. AT 4:15 P. M.

Everyone is weclome, so come and be the guest of

Speedway Service Station

Chrysler - Plymouth - Fargo, Dealers

MACLEOD, ALBERTA

LICENSED
17
Crush

CHAPTER ONE

Anything for a Buck

I will end unemployment or perish in the attempt.

R. B. Bennett, election campaign of 1930

The strange and terrifying thing about the Depression was that there was too much of almost everything. Too much food. In Prince Edward Island potatoes were left rotting in the ground, and on the prairies wheat was burned because it was not worth shipping. Too many houses. There were vacant houses on every street and you could rent a good-sized one for $10 a month. Too many automobiles. Factories could turn out 400,000 a year but only 40,000 were bought in 1932. Too many men for the jobs that needed doing. There was too much of everything, in fact, except jobs and money.

There are as many explanations for the Depression as there are economists and historians to analyze the data. In the 1920s Canada reached a high level of production in farm produce, forest products and manufactured goods. Every industry was expanding, mostly on credit. The same thing was happening in the United States and in other countries upon which Canada depended for trade. It appears that many people became frightened by this credit-based expansion, and suddenly put the brakes on by stopping investment. Instead of buying stocks enthusiastically, they began to sell, and the more they sold the more frightened everyone became.

In October of 1929 fright turned to panic, and the New York stock market crashed. The era of expansion ended abruptly. Governments, industry, banks and individuals stopped spending, stopped investing, stopped lending, stopped expanding. Money stopped moving in its normal way. World trade collapsed. This process fed on itself until it produced economic stagnation.

The prosperity of the twenties had been largely artificial, based on easy credit, high hopes and the need to supply Europe with exports until it had fully recovered from World War I. Canadian industries and agriculture had over-expanded, building up enormous capacity. Huge supplies of food, newsprint, minerals, raw materials of all kinds, glutted world markets. Europe and the United States could not absorb all the products Canada had to offer. World trade in the thirties declined by more than 50 per cent. The world economy stagnated for a decade and, because Canada was so dependent on foreign trade, Canadians suffered as badly as people anywhere.

It took some time after the stock market crash in 1929 for the economy to grind to a near halt. The worst years of the Depression were 1931 through 1933. The price of wheat dropped below 40 cents a bushel and farm incomes in the prairie provinces dropped from $363 million in 1928 to

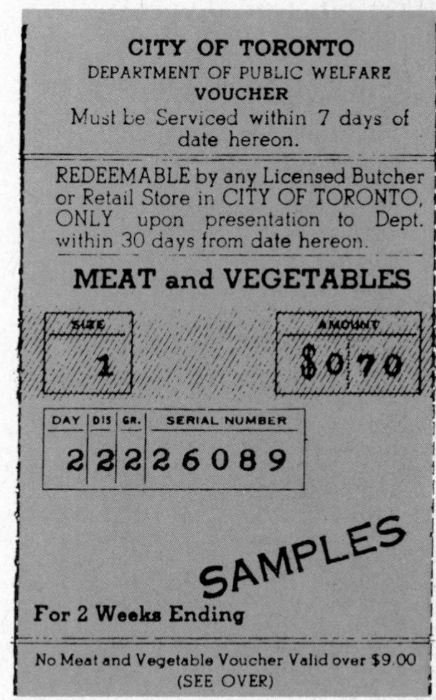

CITY OF TORONTO
DEPARTMENT OF PUBLIC WELFARE
VOUCHER
Must be Serviced within 7 days of date hereon.

REDEEMABLE by any Licensed Butcher or Retail Store in CITY OF TORONTO, ONLY upon presentation to Dept. within 30 days from date hereon.

MEAT and VEGETABLES

SIZE	AMOUNT
1	$0 70

DAY	DIS	GR.	SERIAL NUMBER
2	2	2	26089

SAMPLES

For 2 Weeks Ending

No Meat and Vegetable Voucher Valid over $9.00 (SEE OVER)

For many, relief vouchers were the only form of money in the bleak days.

Opposite page: *Anything for a buck! The depression years brought out the best and worst in people and society. Some sold anything they could from door to door, others hung around streetcorners on Skid Road, looking for the money to buy the next meal.*

minus $10,728,000 in 1931. From 1928 to 1932 the value of Canada's agricultural exports fell from $783 million to $253 million; exports of wood products fell from $289 million to $131 million. Trade picked up some in the mid-thirties and in the industrial areas of Ontario and Quebec the Depression was easing by that time. But on the prairies drought, dust storms and grasshoppers steadily worsened, and in the Maritimes the price of fish remained low. For Canadians in these areas, the Depression lingered until the effects of the war boom began to be felt in the early 1940s.

Not once in the ten years from 1930 to 1940 did the number of unemployed drop below 10 per cent of the work force, not even counting farmers. In 1933, 26.6 per cent of all wage-earners were unemployed. Every occupation was affected, from plumbers to philosophers. A chartered accountant with many years of experience felt lucky to get a job as a part-time attendant at a miniature golf course. One commercial artist who had been out of work for two years got a night job as a short order cook in a tiny restaurant for $6 a week plus meals.

NOTICE

In the absence of the leader of the Marchers at the Stadium Friday morning, the following notice was handed by the Railway Companies' representatives to Bert Canaven, who stated that he was qualified to receive it and would undertake to see that it got to the leader of the Relief Camp Strikers:

REGINA, 14th JUNE, 1935.

To Whom It It May Concern:

We are instructed to inform you that no person or persons will be permitted to further ride on the trains of the Canadian National Railways or on the trains of the Canadian Pacific Railway without authority or without holding proper transportation entitling such person or persons to do so.

It is requested that you will accept this notice and refrain from unlawfully boarding or riding on the trains of either Railway Company, and that you will notify and instruct those that may be associated with you or under your directions not to unlawfully board or ride on any train of either Railway Company.

We are further instructed to inform you that if you or those associated with you further persist in unlawfully riding on the trains of either Railway Company, the proper authorities will give every assistance and use every means available to ensure that the law in this respect is observed.

You are requested to disperse and return to your respective homes. If you will do this the Railway Companies will take up with the Dominion authorities the question of providing some means by which you can so return.

THE CANADIAN NATIONAL RAILWAYS.
THE CANADIAN PACIFIC RAILWAY.

To CNR and CPR officials, "riding the rails" was a serious offense. Both companies employed "bulls" to guard the freight-trains, but for thousands of men – and some women – a free ride was worth a night in the "clink" if somewhere across the country there was a job to be had.

the luxury of being sick

Nine men hiked eleven miles for one job on a farm, only to learn that thirty-nine others had been there ahead of them. Even registered nurses, perennially in short supply, often could find no work. Hospitals had empty beds because many people could not afford the luxury of being sick. A large number of nurses trained during the Depression did not find regular work until the war broke out in 1939.

School teachers throughout Saskatchewan and the Maritimes who had contracted to run a rural school for $300 a year found that there was no money in the community to pay them. They worked for their board or, if married, received direct government relief.

The unemployed tried everything. Thousands sold insurance on commission. After selling their relatives and friends, however, most of them gave up. The streets were full of men trying to sell books, vacuum cleaners, brushes, baby pictures, anything that could be carried from door to door. Sometimes a housewife who had no money would at least give the salesman something to eat before sending him on his way. Others, affected by that vague fear the "haves" often feel for the "have-nots," would not even answer the door.

Riding the rails!

It was easy to recognize an unemployed man, no matter how hard he tried to hide the fact. His homemade haircut was ragged around the edges. The collars and cuffs of his shirt had been carefully turned to put the frayed edges inside. His cigarette case, a relic of better days, was usually filled with homemade cigarettes manufactured on an ingenious gadget a foot-long and then cut with a razor blade into the length of "tailor mades."

Those who were secure and comfortably employed seemed to resent and fear those without jobs. To be idle was to be shiftless – that's what everybody had been taught, and it was impossible to change that thinking in a year. To many, any non-worker was simply a bum. The most tragic waste of the decade was the youth. Nobody needed them; nobody wanted them. By 1936, two-thirds of the young people entering the work force could not find steady employment. There was always a more experienced applicant for any new job.

The unemployed began to wander in search of greener pastures. Hitchhiking was unknown in the thirties; indeed there were few cars on the roads. The only way to get across Canada was to steal a ride on the freight trains. Riding the rails! Almost every young man tried it, most not realizing the experience they were in for.

Fed up with low pay, lack of teaching equipment and the cold, miserable school rooms of Saskatchewan, one young school teacher decided in the summer of 1934 to head for Vancouver. He helped buy gas for a friend who was driving his Ford to the coast and, with some difficulty, they managed to get to British Columbia. The provincial authorities had set up guards along the border to keep out transients, but he was well dressed and had enough money to get through.

Vancouver, he soon discovered, was full of hungry men. He applied everywhere for a job, but employers laughed at his naiveté. By late August his money was gone and the only way to get back to Saskatchewan and his teaching job was to ride the rails. Dressed in a natty white shirt and grey flannels, he went down to the main station in Vancouver and innocently asked a railway policeman, "Is that freight going to Saskatoon?"

The policeman grabbed him, gave him a hefty boot in the trousers and sent him on his way. As the train began to move, he sprinted after it, grabbed hold of the metal ladder and climbed to the top of the car.

twelve of them women

He found himself on the top of a freight car travelling at thirty miles an hour and picking up speed. It was cold and it looked like rain. Just outside the city the train stopped for coal and water and about eighty more transients joined him, twelve of them women. These were the experienced travellers. Each wore about three layers of clothing, a tight cap and a pack with at least some food in it. Because of his unorthodox dress, they were suspicious of the young teacher and would have nothing to do with him.

Soon the train started its long, twisty climb up the Fraser Valley. It was cold and windy, and a slight rain had begun. He lay down on the two-foot

An old oil drum is the stove and yesterday's bad news the wallpaper in this Quebec "living room."

Mean Streets

Not all the streets of the hungry thirties were like these, but from coast to coast the signs of hard times replaced symbols of the previous decade's prosperity. Until the desperation of the hungry, unemployed and destitute erupted in protest, scenes such as these were a constant reminder to all that their own plight could get worse.

A native of New Brunswick's Miramichi drives through town in a cheap and ingenious vehicle. The cost of gasoline rendered cars useless–if creditors hadn't already repossessed them.

Lines at the doors of soup kitchens queued around the block-this one at Port Arthur.

No, it isn't moving day. Tenants, like this Montreal family, who couldn't meet the rent were simply evicted. Those in private homes faced the ever-present threat of foreclosure.

The unemployed used various means to attract attention and a handout. This placard-wearing Toronto youth found a "mark" with his sad but common story.

With the Model A out of gas, all these farmhands of Dauphin, Man., could do was sit on the running board, smoke and wait for rain.

An open-air relief depot at Vancouver's city dump. Between 1931 and 1937, all levels of government spent $813 million for relief.

Room, Board & 20¢ a Day

In 1932 the Department of National Defense established a system of work camps in the country to provide jobs for unemployed single men. Strict in discipline, scarce on pleasure, the relief camps quickly turned into hotbeds of dissent and protest.

Checking in: standard issue of clothes and a number.

Meal time: a ladle of porridge, soup or stew.

wide catwalk that ran along the top of each car, clutching the sides to keep from falling off. When this would not work, he went forward, jumping from car to car until he came to the water tank behind the engine. This seemed to be a better location, lower and somewhat protected from the wind. Then the train went through a tunnel. The engine spewed out smoke and red hot cinders which hit the top of the tunnel and rained down on top of him. He could not escape because the tunnel roof was so low.

After three nights and three days the train reached Edmonton. It was met by a gang of railway police who herded the transients together, arrested them and sent the young teacher and his fellow-travellers to a work camp for sixty days.

The majority of transients found their way into the larger cities because there, theoretically, were the best chances for a job. Vancouver was the sanctuary sought by most prairie wanderers. The streets of Vancouver were cluttered with transients. They hung around the docks and scrounged over-ripe bananas from the unloading boats. They stood in line at Salvation Army hostels and religious missions. They gathered around fires under bridges to keep out of the cold and rain. And they panhandled on the street.

"Panhandling" explained a reluctant practitioner, "is a degrading and guilt-ridden experience. The first time is the worst. You must overcome your life-long feeling of self-respect and pride. It takes a considerable gnawing in the stomach to make you take those few steps towards your 'mark,' accost him and make your audacious request. I think it's as much the idea of interfering with another man's privacy, of imposing yourself upon him."

Throughout the thirties, reluctant panhandlers practised their art across the land, and gathered wherever prospects were best. Many congregated in Toronto, sleeping on steel bunks in the old St. Lawrence Hall, which had once been the main

Work: 8 hours a day building roads in the boondocks.

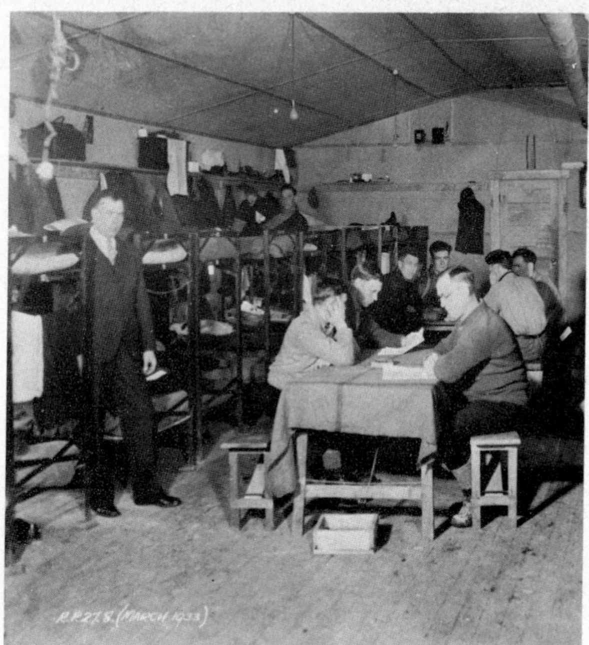

Leisure: card games or letters home; no politics allowed.

Hear the Reply of the authorities to Strikers' Delegation requesting immediate Relief and opening of negotiations on counter-proposals to Bennett Government's offer of Concentration Camps

MASS MEETING TONIGHT

Market Square 8 p.m.

(If wet will be held in Stadium)

Several Speakers representing local organizations will address the crowd

Winnipeg Strike Camp situation will be outlined. Latest developments will be given

Strikers' Funds are Completely Depleted

Support the Strikers and Force the authorities to grant immediate Relief

July 1, 1935: the relief workers strike.

showplace for the rich. Because Toronto was the centre of Ontario manufacturing and finance and, hence, had more prosperous people than some other centres, pickings were relatively good.

In the eastern provinces, young people customarily went south across the border when times were bad. The United States had the same problems, however, and wanted no more men to feed. With the Canadian fishing industry hard hit, the pulp and paper mills closing and mining in a slump, the young Maritime unemployed now also found the border closed to them by special emergency regulations.

Thousands took to the road during the thirties. Nobody knows exactly how many for no statistics were kept. Nor does anybody know how many were injured in falls from freights, got pneumonia sleeping in cold hobo camps, lay moaning at night with toothache or bellies swelled by appendicitis, or were assaulted by older, more experienced knights of the road.

Municipal records and memories of officials do show, however, that little was done for them. The chief preoccupation of the local authorities was to move them on. Some communities provided them with a berth for the night in the local jail or town hall, and sometimes a breakfast before they left. In Montreal, *L'Assistance Publique* reported serving more than 6,000 men during the first six months of 1930. They were young and old, unshaven and poorly dressed, and all were dreadfully hungry. During the next three years, the situation grew steadily worse.

In 1932, partly to alleviate unemployment and partly to ease the potential threat of trouble from thousands of young unemployed men roaming the city streets, the federal government established work camps throughout the country for single, homeless men. The camps were under the control of the Department of National Defence. Under army officers and wearing army-type fatigues, thousands of young men worked eight hours a day

How the Other Side Lived

While almost a quarter of the work force grovelled for jobs, many of the affluent noticed few changes in their life-style. They still spent their summers at cottages or resorts and their money on radio sets, movies, *Mayfair* magazine, or dancing and dining at the Vancouver or Royal York.

This 1930 chauffeur-driven Cadillac belongs to John David Eaton. That's him in the back with his bride.

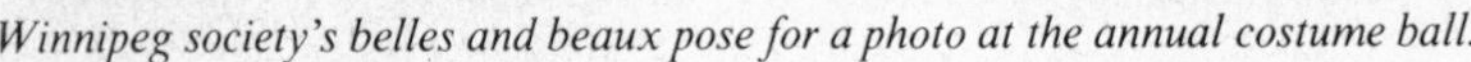

Winnipeg society's belles and beaux pose for a photo at the annual costume ball.

Men's two-piece bathing suits were still the style at Chateau Lake Louise.

on roads, bridges, municipal projects, forestry chores, historic sites, harbours, airfields, anything that needed doing. In return they received food, clothing, lodging and 20 cents a day.

The work camps were a stop gap at best. They succeeded in taking thousands of unemployed young men off the city streets and out of the hobo camps, but did little more. Many of the men were doing work for which they had little aptitude or training. Young men saw their lives passing by with little hope of getting ahead. Some resented the fact that they were under the authority of the military. As one man put it: "It gave you some idea of what a forced labour camp would be like."

If the work camps left much to be desired as a solution to unemployment, government relief was just as unsatisfactory in easing the nation's hunger. Between 1931 and 1937, $813 million in relief money was disbursed by various levels of government. The federal government paid one-third or more of the cost, the province and municipality paid the balance. The system was administered by the municipality. The mechanics of relief were simple enough. The applicant had to go personally to the relief office, stand in line and prove he or she was in need. Vouchers that could be exchanged for food, clothing and fuel were given to successful applicants.

surrender driver's licences

Because relief was administered locally, however, variations did exist. Applicants usually had to produce proof of residence; although the qualifying period was seldom less than six months, in Montreal it was three consecutive years. None of the thousands of men riding freight cars across the country could qualify because they were never in one place long enough. Applicants in Ontario were usually required to surrender driver's licences or licence plates in order to ensure that the relief money would not be used to support an automobile. Any recipient in Saskatchewan who purchased beer or liquor would invariably have their aid cut off.

Everything connected with the system was humiliating. Many of the officials doling out relief adopted a righteous attitude and looked upon those lining up for help as a shiftless and lazy lot. They dished out the vouchers as though they were parting with their own money, fixing the recipient with a withering stare. Anyone using the vouchers to pay for something was immediately identified as being "on the dole."

"relief" and "pogey"

The unemployed could put up with humiliation. What really hurt was that relief was never enough. A family of five living in Ontario in 1932 needed a minimum of $6 to $7 per week for food. In Toronto, where relief payments were relatively high, the weekly food allowance for a family of seven was $6.93. In the small rural areas of Quebec, however, a family of five received about $3.25 for food. Newfoundlanders received 6 cents worth of food a day for each member of the family, and some of them literally starved to death. Although children all over the country were kept home from school because they had no clothes, clothing relief was given grudgingly only by a few municipalities. Furthermore, some of the rural municipalities throughout the country had no money for relief at all.

"Relief" and "pogey" became opprobrious words. There were those who proudly asserted that they were *never* on relief, and others who, after holding out as long as they could, were forced shamefully to admit that they *were.* Thus was the population divided into good guys and bad guys.

Those paying for relief through their taxes came gradually to resent it more and more, and

Elegant St. Andrews-By-The-Sea. Rates were scaled down to $8 per day, and golfers flocked to the course to test their skill in the sport fad of the day.

MINIMUM FOOD SUPPLY FOR 1 WEEK

For a Family of 2 Adults and 3 Children over 2 Years
13c. per person per day

Food	Unit Price	Cost
Milk	.08	$1 12
FRUITS AND VEGETABLES		
Apples (Fresh) or	.05 lb.	
Evaporated Apples and	.13 lb	
Canned Fruit: (Peaches, Pears, Plums)	.12 tin	.25
Tomatoes	.10 tin	.30
Potatoes	.01 lb.	.15
Cabbage	.02 lb.	.06
Onions	.03 lb.	.03
Carrots, Beets, Turnips	.01½ lb.	.15
BREAD, CEREALS AND LEGUMES		
Bread (½ whole wheat)	.06 loaf	.60
Rolled Oats or Cracked Wheat	.04 lb.	.12
Rice, Macaroni, Tapioca or Barley	.05 lb	.05
Flour	.02 lb.	.06
Beans, dried	.03 lb.	.03
Peas, dried	.04 lb.	.04
FATS, SUGARS		
Butter	.24 lb	.48
Shortening	.16 lb.	.08
Sugar	.07 lb.	.14
Molasses	.10 pt.	.10
MEAT AND MEAT SUBSTITUTES		
Beef	.13 lb.	.39
Fish (Dried Cod)	.05 lb	.05
Pork or Beef Liver	.10 lb	.05
Cheese	.14 lb.	.07
Eggs	.40 doz	.10
Peanut Butter	.16 lb	.08

The Minister of Agriculture issued this brochure in 1933 advising housewives how to feed a family of five for 13¢ per person per day.

government spending became a constant complaint of editorial writers. In a 1934 editorial entitled "An Axe for the Tax," *Maclean's* magazine moaned that the total spending of all governments – municipal, provincial and federal – had reached the incredible total of $1 billion!

Besides the official relief all neatly bound up in red tape, concerned private citizens provided great quantities of voluntary relief. Hundreds of freight cars of food and clothing were shipped to the prairies for distribution to needy families. Included, among other things, were windfall apples, good cheddar cheese from Ontario and dried cod from the Maritimes. Many prairie dwellers had never seen dried cod, however, and did not know how to cook it. They dumped it straight into the pan and tried to fry it. The result was a hard, crusted, stinking, inedible mess.

butter for 20 cents a pound

It would be a great mistake to assume that everybody was out of work during the Depression. Many of the four-fifths of the labour force that were still employed were actually better off than they had ever been. Eggs sold for 5 to 10 cents a dozen, a whole dressed chicken for 25 cents, butter for 20 cents a pound, and meat from as low as two pounds for a quarter. Rents were down, and a good suit of clothing cost $25. A man with a steady job in a department store was well off.

The most secure and sought-after jobs were those involving the basic necessities of life. It was a lucky man who had a job delivering bread from door to door. One fifty-year-old man who had owned a successful retail store before the Depression put all his business acumen and energy into securing a job delivering milk. When the dairy assured him they had all the drivers they needed and a long waiting list of younger men, he went around from house to house soliciting new customers. He persuaded forty people to agree to take milk from him if he could get a route. He presented the dairy with the list of customers, got the job, and was elated to get up at five o'clock in the morning six days a week to make his deliveries.

Government jobs were also very attractive, first because they were very secure and second because the wages had not been cut as drastically as they had in private industry. Municipal police forces, fire departments and even sanitation departments, which might otherwise have had difficulty recruiting workers, had waiting lists with hundreds of names. And the person lucky enough to land such a job, either through pull or connivance, made sure that he held on to it.

as low as $3.80 a week

Naturally, there were plenty of jobs that were little better than relief. One writer wrote a daily 15-minute serial for radio about an heroic dog for $12.00 a week, when he was paid at all. A Royal Commission on Price Spreads in 1935 found that furniture factory workers were averaging 464 dollars a year and that chain store clerks were getting as low as $3.80 a week. Perhaps the worst conditions existed among women and children doing piece work sewing at home for garment companies. One woman in the east end of Toronto crocheted baby jackets for $1.65 a dozen, which meant that by working all day she could not earn more than 27 cents.

For almost all Canadians, the Depression was a time of deep confusion, a time when their hopes and prayers, fears and frustrations focussed on jobs. Political leaders argued over how to create or improve them. Those who had them were afraid of losing them. The unemployed were desperate for work of any kind. And those who struggled all day for 27 cents dreamed of a more equitable share of Canada's wealth.

Get Rich Quick! Hard times brought with them a spate of easy-money schemes. The alluring pitch that promised something-for-nothing enticed millions who, on their incomes, could afford little more than the basics.

Magazines 1930-1939

Had it not been for the occasional hard times story, a retrospective look at Canada's national magazines might conclude, "What Depression?" *Maclean's* and *Chatelaine* patterned their covers in the Rockwell style of *The Saturday Evening Post,* the most successful American weekly of the decade; day-dreamy glamour girls adorned the covers of *National Home Monthly*; vignettes of happy home-life sold *Canadian Home Journal* to women whose hardest job was making ends meet. *Mayfair,* the magazine of the elite, carried "who's who" articles; *The Farmer* went to 100,000 rural families in Eastern Canada; and *Liberty* carried the sensational American stories under its "Printed in Canada" weekly wrapper.

Winnipeg's Bannatyne and Dagmar claimed NHM *was "Canada's Greatest Magazine."*

Consolidated Press of Toronto devoted The Farmer *to farming in the East.*

Maclean's *came twice a month for 10¢ a copy under H. Napier Moore's editorship.*

Domestic tips and human interest fiction from CHJ *before* Chatelaine *took it over.*

MAYFAIR

AUGUST : 1938

SUMMER SPORTS
TRAVEL · SOCIETY

25c

Suitcase stickers from Canada's fashionable hotels and resorts highlight this summer issue of Maclean-Hunter's Montreal publication for the well-dressed, well-travelled and well-bred.

"Liberty – for liberals with common sense." Stories were prefaced by "reading times."

Editor B.H. Sanders blended strong views on women's roles with practical home items.

CHAPTER TWO

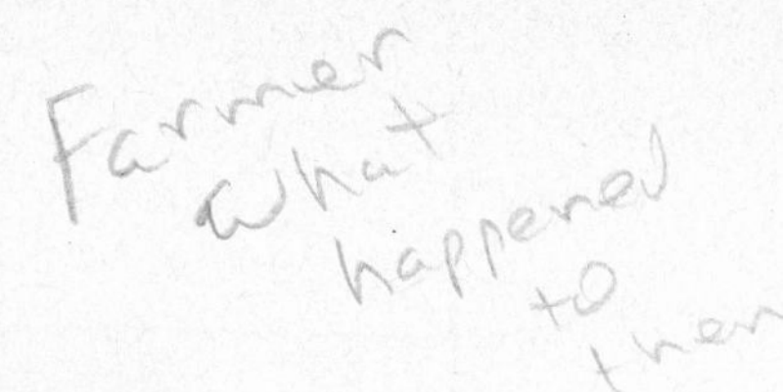

The Land Dries to Dust

There were worse things than being on relief... worst of all was being a farmer in the Dust Bowl.

James H. Gray in *The Winter Years*

The first sign of trouble had appeared in 1928 when the annual amount of precipitation was in many locations less than half of what it had been the previous year. At Regina it dropped from 14.54 inches to 5.98. Only the subsoil moisture from the previous wet years helped produce an average crop. But it was dry again in 1929 and the subsoil moisture was just about gone. The drought cycle was upon them.

In the spring of 1930, prairie farmers, like everyone else in Canada, were worried but optimistic. The price of wheat had fallen lower than anyone could remember, but from what everybody told them – Eastern industrialists, politicians, even their own Wheat Pool officials – this was a temporary condition. R.B. Bennett was saying that, if elected, he would "blast" Canada's way into the world markets, and Eastern manufacturers warned that a let-down in buying could precipitate a recession. So the farmers went ahead and planted big crops.

There is always plenty of wind on the plains. The average wind speed at Swift Current is sixteen miles per hour. And the six-horse team or tractor pulling the seeder always kicks up a cloud of dust. In 1930, however, the dust blew differently. It picked up without any disturbance and swept across the flat fields in a constant face-pestering stream. When the grain came up, the dust abated somewhat, but it was bad again in the fall.

That winter was a particularly mild one with little snow, and the dust began to stir early the following March. By mid-spring of 1931, the full-blown dust storm had hit the plains.

It was worse than a blizzard. People could stay indoors during blizzards, but dust storms came in spring and early summer when the farmer had to be on the land. Coming in from the field after a day's harrowing or seeding, a man's face was as black as coal and the dust had sifted through his clothing and under his goggles. His eyes were bloodshot and sore.

Dust sifted in everywhere. There was no way to keep it out. It piled up in little drifts on window sills and floors, saturated curtains with a dirty greyness, got into the clothes closets and cupboards. It even got into the food. During one particularly bad dust storm when you could not see across the street, one Saskatchewan man came home to find his wife and child in bed with wet cloths over their faces. It was not safe to breathe the air.

The effect on the land was devastating. The fine top soil lifted off and blew away, often taking the newly planted seed with it. Jim Boak, who

R. B. Bennett makes the wild west wild. Farmers raged in August 1930 when the new PM's tariff increases discriminated against the West.

Opposite page: Young Canadian *by Winnipeg artist Charles Comfort one of the strongest artistic statements of the depression years.*

MASS
MEETING
VARIETY THEATRE
SUN. DEC. 11
AT 8 p.m.

Subject: The Need For A Xmas Clothing Allowance

SPEAKERS from:
Unemployed Union
Unemployed Ex-Servicemen's Assn.
Women's Unemployed Assn.

All Aldermen Invited to Attend and Speak

ALL THE PUBLIC ARE INVITED

–MOST IMPORTANT–

Protest groups cropped up in cities throughout the West. Resenting the handouts from the East, the jobless organized ad-hoc to air complaints.

In mid-spring of '31, one of history's worst dust storms hit the prairies. Frustrated farmers left by the hundreds.

farmed near Meacham, Saskatchewan, claimed that so much of his neighbour's summer fallow blew onto his field it buried his crop and he had to reseed the field. "I swear my field was three inches higher after the blow," he contended.

Dust filled the ditches, buried fences, and drifted half way up the barn door. It cut off the tender new shoots as they poked their way up through the ground. The wind gouged giant holes out of the best of the fields. Farmers joked that they could throw a gopher up in the air and it would dig a hole before it hit the ground.

Along with the dust and the drought came their two evil step-children – grasshoppers and Russian thistle.

The grasshoppers indigenous to the prairies are not the fabled locusts that descend on a crop and destroy it overnight. The roadside grasshopper and the stubble grasshopper are born and bred beside the fields they will eventually eat. In the early spring, the eggs hatch into little, black, wingless nymphs that look exactly like adult grasshoppers and have tremendous appetites. They begin eating the grain as it pokes up. As the grain grows so do the grasshoppers, feeding on it at every stage. When the hopper finally reaches maturity and has wings, it attaches itself to the grain stem just below the head, sucks it dry and cuts off the head leaving a worthless stalk.

The grasshoppers were so thick they clogged the radiators of cars, made the roads slippery and, some say, even chewed the clothing on the line. Chickens and turkeys gobbled up grasshoppers by the thousand, giving a vile taste to their eggs and flesh. There were no sprays. Sawdust soaked in paris green was spread round the edges of the fields but it had little effect.

The only thing that will effectively control the

Abandoned farmhouses dotted the Saskatchewan landscape. Many of these still stand as a lasting monument to hard times.

grasshoppers is a cold, wet spring. There were no cold, wet springs during the thirties.

Russian thistle also thrives on drought. Its tremendous root system seeks deep into the soil for every drop of water, while its thread-like leaves lose little through transpiration. When the wheat is stunted for lack of water, the Russian thistle grows tall, shutting it off from the sun, crowding it out. When the thistle ripens, the whole plant breaks off and rolls like tumbling mustard across the field, spreading millions of seeds from the long, slender flower spikes. The thistle piles up against fences and barns, often to a depth of twenty feet.

Some of the greatest hardships of the Depression were borne by Canadian farmers. Nothing they raised was worth much. In 1933, Wallace Gallagher took a truckload of cattle from Laurel to Toronto and got 4 cents a pound for the best of them, 3.5 cents for the rest. Gallagher had a bumper potato crop that same year and considered himself lucky to get 15 cents for a ninety-pound bag. Some of his neighbours weren't so lucky – they hauled their potatoes to the swamp to keep them from rotting in the bins. In British Columbia, 8,000 tons of tomatoes were ploughed under.

Of all the farmers, however, the hardest hit were the wheat farmers on the prairies. While those in Ontario, Quebec, British Columbia and the Maritimes had a diversity of crops and often some market for their fruit and vegetables close at hand, the prairie farmer was strictly a grower of grain, principally wheat, and with world markets gone he had no place to sell it.

In addition, the West had a "debt" economy. Each spring the farmer risked everything he had or could borrow on the chance of having a good crop. He bought more land and mortgaged it; he bought new implements on credit; he borrowed cash from

Saskatchewan

Saskatchewan, the land of snow,
Where winds are always on the blow,
Where people sit with frozen toes,
And why we stay here no one knows.

Saskatchewan, Saskatchewan,
There's no place like Saskatchewan.
We sit and gaze across the plains,
And wonder why it never rains,
And Gabriel blows his trumpet sound,
He says: The rain, she's gone around.

Our pigs are dyin' on their feet
Because they have no feed to eat,
Our horses, though of bronco race,
Starvation stares them in the face.

The milk from cows has ceased to flow,
We've had to ship 'em East, you know,
Our hens are old and lay no eggs,
Our turkeys eat grasshopper legs.

But still we love Saskatchewan,
We're proud to say we're native ones,
So count your blessings drop by drop,
Next year we'll have a bumper crop.

Swift Current, Saskatchewan's Bill Smith composed this ditty to the tune of "Beulah Land," proving that at least one of the survivors never lost his sense of humour.

Faces of the Prairie Depression

The faces of the Prairie Depression tell a story that no words can tell. Drought, grasshoppers, dust storms, Russian thistle, credit shortages and small incomes turned the optimism of the good years to total despair.

Unemployed drifters crossed the prairies in empty boxcars, setting up camps along the railway tracks.

With no money for gas, farmers took the engines out of cars, hitched their livestock to the bumper, and rode into town in their "Bennett Buggies."

All the students in the front row of this Winnipeg class wear relief boots.

Children of the prairie depression – a story told in one picture.

Families packed up all their earthly goods, left their farms and moved on toward better land. The wheat belt lost over 25% of its population.

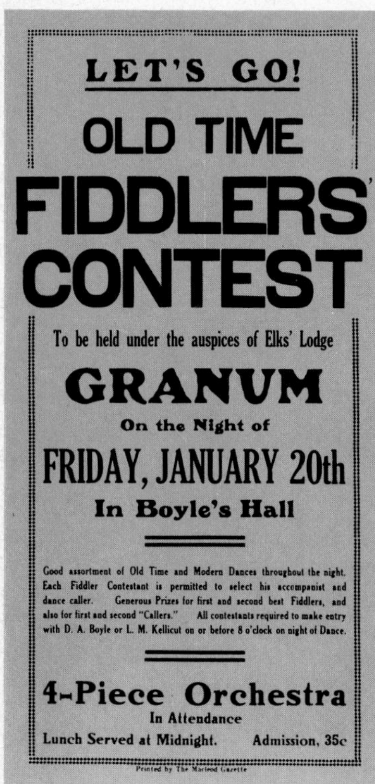

Entertainment for a Friday night with Granum, Alberta's top fiddlers.

the benevolent banker to see him through the long summer when there was no income. After harvesting his crop in the fall, he paid off most of his debts.

When the Depression hit, credit dried up like the slough behind the barn. Nobody had any money to lend, and creditors demanded their due. The bank manager's smile turned to a worried frown and then to an accusing grimace. The genial salesmen did not come around any more, and the implement companies sent crisp letters demanding payment or the return of their machinery.

more cardboard than leather

Prairie winters are the most cruel in Canada. The wind blows incessantly and the temperature frequently drops 50 degrees below zero fahrenheit. During the Depression, clothing wore out and there was no money for new garments. Men tied gunny sacks around their feet in lieu of overshoes; children wore old socks instead of mittens. Old buffalo coats were resurrected from the barn where they had been buried for years. Empty flour sacks were used to make underwear and even dresses. Trousers and overalls became a mass of patches. Shoes had more cardboard than leather in their soles. Children were kept home from school because they had no clothes to wear. School boards had no money for coal or teachers' salaries. Friendly, warm, hospitable people found themselves becoming mean and niggardly through want.

In 1937 there was more dust, more Russian thistle, more army worms, more grasshoppers than ever before, and less rain! Everything in the southern part of the prairies dried up. Poplar groves and even caragana hedges could not stand the drought. Large sloughs that had never been dry in living memory lost all their water and dust rose from their bottoms. Many farmers had no crop at all, and the average for the entire province of Saskatchewan, including some fair crops in the northern region, was 2.7 bushels to the acre.

In some municipalities 90 per cent of the farmers were on relief that year. There was not even any hay or coarse grain to feed starving livestock. Municipalities brought in tons of relief hay from Ontario and British Columbia, and many farmers made hundred-mile trips into the northern part of the province to buy hay on their own.

Many southern Saskatchewan farmers finally gave up. They left the farms that they had spent years building up from homesteads, loaded their belongings onto hayracks and drove away. Many went north into the Prince Albert or Meadow Lake areas where the soil was poorer but the moisture more plentiful. Here some of them were able to make some money growing alfalfa seed, which would yield up to 600 pounds to the acre and sold in the United States for 26 cents a pound.

"Bennett Buggies" and "Anderson Carts"

Others left the province altogether. Some went back to Ontario; 5,000 settled in the Fraser Valley in British Columbia; and others even went back to Britain. Between 1931 and 1937, Alberta lost 21,000 people, Manitoba almost 34,000 and Saskatchewan 66,000.

Throughout the drought, dust and disasters, however, most of the western farmers somehow "made do." Because they could not afford gasoline or licences for their cars, they removed the engines, attached a wagon pole and whippletrees to the front, and hitched on a team of horses. Much to the chagrin of the man they had elected prime minister in 1930, they called these ingenious contraptions "Bennett Buggies." A smaller version of the same rig was called the "Anderson Cart," after the Conservative premier of Saskatchewan.

As the Depression lengthened, more and more Bennett Buggies were seen on the dusty roads, pulled by half-starved horses, taking people to church, to town for shopping, to sports gatherings, wherever they had once travelled in cars.

Throughout the cold crisp prairie winters, another ingenious contraption that could be seen skimming over the snow carrying farmers, doctors, Fuller brush men and veterinarians was the covered sleigh or jumper, a light, handy rig of plywood built to fit on a set of runners. The jumper had a narrow glass window in the front which could be slid back and forth to permit the reins to come through, a narrow back window to give the driver rear vision and a tight-fitting door. The most important part of the rig was the small coal-burning stove that sat in one corner with the stovepipe protruding through the roof. With just the slightest fire in the stove, the caravan was snug and warm even in a thirty below blizzard.

boxes of cigars as prizes

The covered sleigh was often used by curlers on their way to all-night bonspiels. It is impossible to overestimate the importance of curling to the western farmer during the thirties. Every town had a curling rink and every able-bodied man and woman curled, from sixteen to seventy, often on the same teams. At school the children played a game of curling with jam tins filled with frozen mud and wire handles stuck in them. As soon as the chores were done in the morning, the farmer would head for town and the rink. There was always some kind of bonspiel going on, with jars of coffee, blankets or boxes of cigars donated by the local merchants as prizes.

Those who were not on the ice were sitting behind the glass partition, watching the game with an intensity and enthusiasm that no hockey game would ever command. Each curler had his or her standing in the community and was carefully rated so that the different rinks could be evenly ba-

Depression Scrips

Forerunners of William Aberhart's Prosperity Certificates of 1936, "depression scrips" were issued in Alberta towns to pay for overdue taxes and beef up the empty municipal coffers.

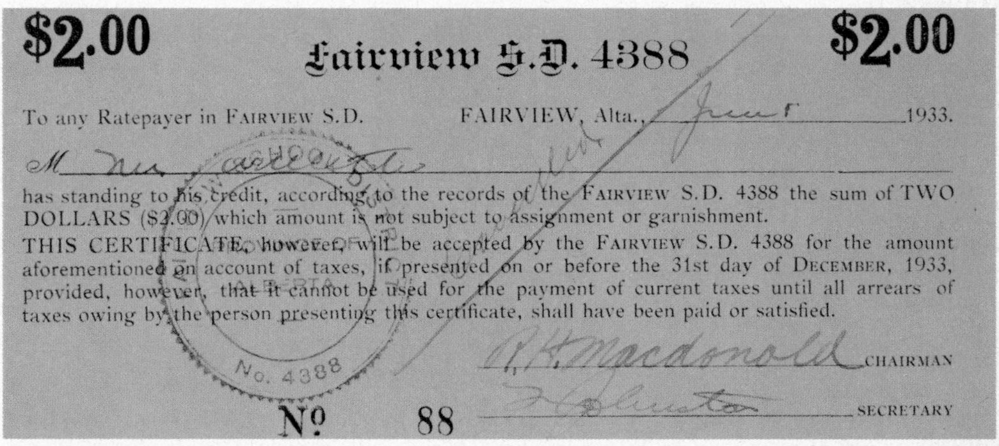

$2.00 Fairview S.D. 4388 $2.00

To any Ratepayer in FAIRVIEW S.D. FAIRVIEW, Alta., 1933.

has standing to his credit, according to the records of the FAIRVIEW S.D. 4388 the sum of TWO DOLLARS ($2.00) which amount is not subject to assignment or garnishment.

THIS CERTIFICATE, however, will be accepted by the FAIRVIEW S.D. 4388 for the amount aforementioned on account of taxes, if presented on or before the 31st day of DECEMBER, 1933, provided, however, that it cannot be used for the payment of current taxes until all arrears of taxes owing by the person presenting this certificate, shall have been paid or satisfied.

CHAIRMAN

No 88 SECRETARY

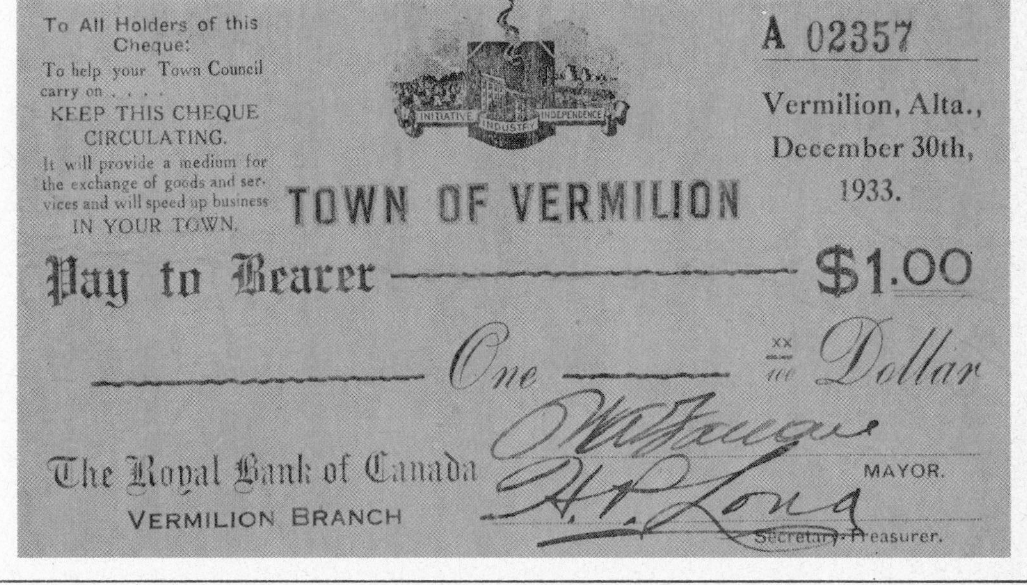

To All Holders of this Cheque:
To help your Town Council carry on . . . .
KEEP THIS CHEQUE CIRCULATING.
It will provide a medium for the exchange of goods and services and will speed up business IN YOUR TOWN.

INITIATIVE INDUSTRY INDEPENDENCE

A 02357

Vermilion, Alta., December 30th, 1933.

TOWN OF VERMILION

Pay to Bearer $1.00

One xx/100 Dollar

The Royal Bank of Canada
VERMILION BRANCH

MAYOR.

Secretary-Treasurer.

J. S. Woodsworth
"A Prophet in Politics"

Minister, social reformer, pacifist, labour leader and parliamentarian, James Shaver Woodsworth was born near Islington, Ontario, in 1874. After his education at Manitoba, Toronto and Oxford Universities, he worked for eighteen years among the immigrants of Winnipeg's North End ghetto. In 1918 he resigned from the church, worked as a longshoreman on Vancouver's waterfront, and he became deeply involved in the problems of labour organization. When the Winnipeg General Strike erupted in May 1919, Woodsworth was one of the leaders arrested. Public outrage and growing support catapulted him into federal politics where he served from 1921 to 1939. Woodsworth's socialist ideals were the foundation of the CCF, its platform, the Regina Manifesto of 1933, and the antecedent of the present New Democratic Party.

lanced. Each shot was scrutinized from the time it left the curler's hand until it reached the "house."

"He's light!" a burly farmer dressed in smock and overalls would boom.

"No, he's heavy!" the United Church minister would contradict.

"He's going to come right through the house."

"Sweep! Dammit. Sweep!"

Long afterward, in the rink or along coffee row in the Chinese cafe, the shots would be gone over again and again.

Farmers, businessmen, doctors and bankers would journey in covered sleighs to a near-by town for the all-night bonspiel. Somebody always brought along a deck of cards for a game of cribbage or smear, and the druggist would sometimes bring a pint or two of grain alcohol flavoured with essence of juniper berries, just in case the stove happened to go out.

The bonspiel was a round robin, knockout draw with the rinks of one town matched against those of the other. Those who were not curling were over in the back of the cafe or in the hotel playing cards, talking curling and drinking the druggist's homemade gin. Each time the team went back on they curled with more confidence and less skill.

"bloated plutocrats" of Eastern Canada

Curling in the thirties was a lot more satisfying than the West's other traditional sport, politics. The great age of farmer protest against the East and Ottawa had been in the 1920s when the Progressives had held the balance of power in the House of Commons. Disunity and the prosperity of the late twenties, however, had killed the Progressive Party and it was not revived in the thirties.

The farmers' co-ops, another attempt to strike a blow against the "bloated plutocrats" of Eastern Canada, also suffered in the thirties from the general lack of business. The greatest of all co-ops, the Wheat Pools, were bankrupt by 1931, had to be bailed out by the Ottawa government and never regained their importance. Everything went wrong in the thirties.

The more things went wrong, though, the more some farmers and teachers and preachers became convinced that capitalism had finally come to the end of its road. The West did give Canada a new and lasting national party when the CCF was founded at Calgary in 1932. A year later the party's Regina Manifesto promised that "No CCF Government will rest until it has eradicated capitalism and put into operation the full programme of socialized planning which will lead to the establishment in Canada of the Co-operative Commonwealth."

frightened by its radicalism

The West also gave the CCF its leaders – J.S. Woodsworth, the saintly ex-clergyman who had long sat for a Winnipeg riding in the House of Commons; M.J. Coldwell, a Regina school teacher who almost lost his job for daring to run as a socialist; and Tommy Douglas, who would eventually become premier of Saskatchewan.

But not yet. For although we think of the CCF as a Depression party, it actually enjoyed little success in the 1930s. Most voters were frightened by its radicalism or, at least, by the "red" brush the old parties regularly tarred the CCF with. The party did best in Saskatchewan – where the Depression was worst – gaining about 25 per cent of the vote and becoming the official Opposition. A few years later the Depression was over, but its memory, plus the hard organizing work of these years, would lead to the election of the first socialist government in North America in Saskatchewan in 1944.

Artists of the Hungry Thirties

Not even the traditionally insular world of art survived the Depression without bearing the weight of social concern and the pinch of tight money. At the National Gallery the 1930 budget of $130,000 was cut to a mere $25,000 for salaries and acquisitions in 1934. Its director, Eric Brown, was confronted by a delegation of 100 angry artists in 1932, protesting the Gallery's lack of support. From 1932 to 1936, only one major Canadian work was added to its collection.

Nevertheless, accustomed to the whims of fate, Canadian artists persisted in their work. Some, like Miller Brittain, Philip Surrey, Paraskeva Clark, André Bieler and Jean-Paul Lemieux, translated their sentiments into works of Social Realism.

Paraskeva Clark, Petroushka, *1937.*
When controversy raged about the social role artists should play, the Russian-born Toronto painter remarked: "Come out from behind the Pre-Cambrian Shield."

Emily Carr, Indian Church, *c. 1930. The thirties saw the pinnacle of her work.*

Philip Surrey, Sunday Afternoon, *1939. The artist's lyrical past is all but lost in the characters at this rural Quebec vigil.*

André Biéler, Before the Auction, *1938. The structure and reality of Quebec life became the dominant theme for the Swiss-born artist.*

Franklin Arbuckle, Saturday Night, *1939. A rare, candid view of a Toronto beer parlour, incisive and satirical.*

CHAPTER THREE

Left, Right & Centre

You cannot go and take the government by the throat . . .

Prime Minister R. B. Bennett to relief strikers' delegation, 1935

During the worst years of the Depression, some desperate and hungry Canadians found themselves considering desperate solutions. One solution was Communism.

The Communist Party of Canada had been organized with great secrecy in a barn near the city of Guelph, Ontario, in May of 1921. The secrecy was necessary. It was just four years after the Russian Revolution, and Canada and the United States, along with many other capitalist countries, were in a state of panic known as the "Big Red Scare."

One of the Party's most eager and dynamic organizers was a thin, short, blue-eyed, rather pleasant looking man named Timothy Buck. In 1910, at the age of nineteen, Buck had come to Canada from his native England as a machinist. He was a confirmed Marxist, having at the tender age of sixteen fallen under the spell of the Scottish socialist, James Keir Hardy. Those who knew Buck describe him as a rather mild, even bland man who wore blue suits and conservative ties. He was a family man, fond of children, dogs and the poetry of Shelley. Underneath this mild exterior, however, was an extremely able, devious and ruthless organizer.

The aims of the new Party were frank and explicit: "Violent defeat of the bourgeoisie, the confiscation of its property, the annihilation of the entire bourgeois governmental apparatus, parliamentary, judicial, military, bureaucratic, administrative, municipal." Since strikes were one of the avowed tools of the Communists, Buck spent much of his time during the lush twenties trying to increase the membership and undercut the labour movement. It was slim pickings. The country, particularly Toronto where the Party had its office, was in a buoyant mood.

In 1924 Buck went to Moscow as a delegate to the Comintern and attended the Lenin School where he was considered a "star pupil." In 1929, when Jack MacDonald was expelled by the Russians as secretary of the Canadian Party for being too soft on capitalism, Tim Buck became the new secretary and leader of the Party. As the lush twenties gave way to the dirty thirties, it was a different story. Communism thrives on poverty, misery and discontent. Everywhere there were unhappy Canadians who were ready to try anything. Tim Buck was ready to promise them anything.

Wherever a group of unemployed gathered together to discuss their problems, in work camps, at protest meetings, on street corners, in pool halls, Tim Buck had a Party representative on hand to turn the conversation toward the overthrow of the

The verdict of the "Workers Jury" in the celebrated 1931 trial of Toronto's Communist leaders is a resounding "NOT GUILTY!"

Opposite page: *"Iron Heel" Bennett goes to the nation via radio with his incredible "New Deal" in 1935.*

Tim Buck
Voice of the Far Left

One of the original members of the Communist Party of Canada, Tim Buck was born in England and came to Canada in 1910 at age nineteen. He was a machinist by trade – vocal, forceful and radical in his views. In 1924 he enrolled at the Lenin School in Moscow, and on returning to Toronto took over the leadership of the Party. Open confrontations punctuated the summer of '31. The headquarters was raided by "Bulldog" Draper's squad and Buck spent three years in the Kingston Pen. In 1934 his "coming-out party" packed the new Maple Leaf Gardens to capacity but the rally was without incident. The ban on Communist activities was lifted in 1936 but votes and public interest had waned. Buck regrouped the faithful again in '43 but the Party's great days were over.

government. There is no doubt that many of the protests and marches that punctuated the thirties grew out of plain frustration and anger and had no Communist connection. There is also no doubt that Tim Buck's lieutenants had a hand in organizing many others.

During one weekend in the fall of 1930, there were at least four major confrontations between police and unemployed throughout the country. In Winnipeg, police stopped a group of marchers on their way to city hall with a list of grievances. In Windsor, 4,000 workers marched to city hall and then to the employment office, with no major trouble. In Montreal, 20,000 marchers were charged by police on motorcycles.

In Toronto that weekend the situation was bad. Trouble had been brewing in Toronto with the Communists for some time. The previous year a gathering led by Jack MacDonald had been broken up at Queen's Park by police on horses. A few heads were bloodied. Now the police were ready for Toronto demonstrators and, when 15,000 of them appeared at city hall, they arrested the first three men who tried to address the crowd, along with nine demonstrators.

"the iron heel of ruthlessness"

The official attitude toward unemployed men or women who gathered together for any purpose had been set by the Bennett government. To R. B. Bennett this was all the work of Communists. To deal with the problem, the federal government dusted off Section 98 of the Criminal Code, an amendment passed during the Winnipeg General Strike in 1919 which made it a crime to belong to any party that advocated change by the use of "force, violence, or physical injury." Bennett had publicly asked "every true Canadian to put the iron heel of ruthlessness against a thing of that sort."

One method of dealing with agitators who were not Canadian citizens was deportation. Between 1930 and 1934, 22,968 persons were deported, many under the provisions of Section 98. Many of them were returned to Britain, but others were shipped to European countries including Italy and Germany, where to be a Communist meant internment in a concentration camp.

carted off to jail

Arrests were frequent. According to Section 98, anyone attending a meeting where a Communist or suspected Communist was speaking could be carted off to jail. The police especially harassed known Communists whose meeting places were open. On August 11, 1931, a series of raids was carried out. One raid on Communist headquarters in Toronto resulted in the arrest of Tim Buck and eight others, including six of Buck's most important lieutenants.

Under the provisions of Section 98, they were charged with being members and acting as members of an unlawful association and with being parties to a seditious conspiracy. The Crown produced as a witness RCMP Sergeant John Leopold, who had worked as an undercover agent within the Communist movement for seven years. Leopold testified that the Party planned to forcefully overthrow governments and institutions.

Largely as a result of his testimony, Tim Buck and all but one of his associates were easily convicted. All were sentenced to prison, including Buck who got a total of five years. An appeal court upheld the conviction and the men were sent to Portsmouth Penitentiary in Kingston.

While they were in jail the Communist Party worked tirelessly for their release, led by former Methodist minister A. E. Smith, head of the Party-sponsored Canadian Labour Defence League. At the same time, RCMP and local police continued to put more and more pressure on the Communists. In the first six months of 1932, according to reports in the Communist newspaper *The Worker,* 132 Communists had been convicted for Party activity, and sentenced to a total of 72 years in jail. During the same period, it reported, 105 raids by police had resulted in the breaking up of 53 meetings and the wounding of 125 "comrades."

The controversy came to a head in the fall of 1932 when the prisoners at Portsmouth rioted and the guards, who claimed that Tim Buck was responsible, went to his cell and shot at him with a pistol and shotguns. This led to inquiries and questions in the House of Commons. It was never made clear why the guards shot at the Communist leader or why, at that range, they missed.

After the shooting, Smith increased his efforts to free the prisoners and, in February of 1933, presented to Prime Minister Bennett a petition with almost 200,000 names demanding the repeal of Section 98. For his pains, Smith himself was arrested and tried for sedition but was acquitted on the evidence of Tim Buck, of all people, who testified that he had indeed been shot at. Shortly after, in 1934, the Communist prisoners were paroled.

17,000 filled Maple Leaf Gardens

Never before had the Communists enjoyed so much attention and publicity. Four thousand cheering supporters met Tim Buck's train in Toronto and carried him out of the station on their shoulders. This was their greatest triumph. A week later, no less than 17,000 people filled Maple Leaf Gardens to applaud Buck as he literally shook his fist in the face of the government and defied them to arrest the whole lot of them under Section 98. Nobody broke up this meeting.

The Communists continued their activities and

Arch Dale vs. R.B.B.

Winnipeg *Free Press* cartoonist Arch Dale's arch-enemy was none other than the prime minister himself. Bennett, a towering, powerful man, was a caricaturist's dream come to power. His election promises and policies were as big a target as the PM himself, and the wry Scotsman had no trouble hitting the mark.

Different Drummers

Protesters in the thirties marched under a dozen different banners, and May Day of any year saw a forest of placards out in public squares. There were communists and relief camp workers, "brown shirts" (Nazis) and "grey suits" (technocrats), prairie farmers and auto workers. It seemed that everyone had a grievance, and no one was prepared to listen. But the demonstrators continued to march to the sounds of different drummers.

Chinese workers in Vancouver lay the blame for 145 deaths at the door of the church.

The Canadian Labour Defence League, a cover for the outlawed Communist Party, mounts an all-out protest in Toronto over Tim Buck's shooting.

The Young Communist League of Vancouver, dramatically dressed in prison stripes, parades through the streets protesting relief camp conditions.

Unemployed workers crowd the steps of Winnipeg's parliament buildings on May Day 1931.

The logo of Adrien Arcand's Nazi Party.

June 1935: Thousands of men, fed up with their life in B.C. relief camps, boarded CPR freights bound for Ottawa. Trouble began when they were stopped at Regina and told to go no farther.

22,000 marched in the May Day Parade in Toronto as late as 1938. Most of the unemployed wanted jobs, however, not a revolution. As more jobs gradually became available in the industrial part of Canada, many men went back to work and others believed that their turn soon would come.

In western Canada where there was little industrial development, no such relief was in sight. Vancouver was hardest hit. The hundreds of thousands of single unemployed males congregated there from the prairie regions and eastern Canada were restless. Wherever there were idle men, there were Communist zealots to offer them a philosophy and a course of action.

"Scanlon's Cossacks"

In Vancouver the Communists regimented the unemployed into gangs of marchers who walked up and down the main streets, peacefully begging but generally disrupting traffic and interfering with the public. The sergeant of police in Vancouver was Jack Scanlon who, with his squad of constables nicknamed "Scanlon's Cossacks," brooked no nonsense from anyone loitering on the streets.

There were continual scuffles, broken heads, arrests and imprisonments. When the unemployed demonstrated in the Hudson's Bay Store and upset glass showcases on the ground floor, the police chased them out and followed the belligerent men into Victory Square. It appeared for a while there would be a full-scale riot until Mayor Gerry McGeer read the Riot Act. McGeer was greatly aided in his attempt to placate the men by a member of the provincial legislature named Harold Winch. A graduate of street fights himself, Winch knew the language of the unemployed, and many times afterward talked men out of fights with reason and good sense.

Much of the Communist organizing was done in the labour camps, where destitute single men slugged all day, moving rock, cutting brush and pushing wheelbarrows for their board and 20 cents. In the long evenings, there was nothing much to do but talk and complain. The Communists, always the best talkers, organized many of them into the Relief Project Workers' Union. The Regina Riot of Dominion Day, 1935, had its beginning in the work camps of British Columbia at the instigation of the RPWU.

The plan was to send thousands of unemployed men on a peaceful march to Ottawa to present their grievances personally to the government. It would not be a march in the real sense, since the men travelled mostly in and on top of freight cars. The initial marchers would be joined by other jobless men as they moved east. The Royal Canadian Mounted Police notified the federal government of the plan. The government, fearing armed revolution, went into a mild state of panic.

On June 14, almost 1,300 marchers arrived in Regina, and the police had orders to stop them there. Without warning Regina found itself with hundreds of angry, frustrated men wandering the streets, begging for handouts and defying the police.

neared the flash point

Trouble was temporarily averted when the unemployed men were persuaded to take up residence in the Exhibition grounds. They were granted permission to hold an orderly tag day on the hot, dry streets of the city. This provided them with enough money to buy food, and they decided to wait there and send a delegation on to Ottawa to present their grievances. They tried to hire trucks to take the delegation on their way, but were refused permission to do this. Enraged, the men turned down the offer of a temporary relief camp in nearby Lumsden and the situation again neared the flash point.

The marchers had now been in Regina for more than two weeks with nothing much to do except listen to the Communists among them explain their rights. On July 1, the Communist leaders organized an open air meeting in downtown Regina where the citizens of the town, most of whom were having a holiday and had no place to go, could listen to their story.

The RCMP and the Regina City Police turned out in force and, using the authority vested in them by Section 98, arrested the first man who got up to speak. Another got up and they arrested him, too. There was shouting and cursing, shoving and punching. Somebody swung a club. Somebody else threw a stone, and the fight was on.

one policeman was killed

With flying billies, sticks, rocks, bottles and fists, it was hard to determine who was hitting whom. Benches were wrecked, street lamps shattered, store windows smashed, and cars overturned. A lot of the local men without jobs and the destitute farmers found five years of frustration and anger bursting from them. Before it was all over, one policeman was killed and scores were injured; over a hundred were arrested and downtown Regina was a trail of broken glass and debris. Premier James G. Gardiner opened talks with the leaders of the marchers and, as a result, most of the men left the city on July 5, in special trains provided by the Saskatchewan government.

The Saskatchewan government blamed the federal government for much of the trouble. A royal commission was appointed to investigate. It concluded that the RCMP and the federal government were blameless and cited the real villain as the Communist influence among the marchers.

As late as 1938, while the newspapers and magazines in Ontario were saying the Depression was over, there were more transients in Vancouver

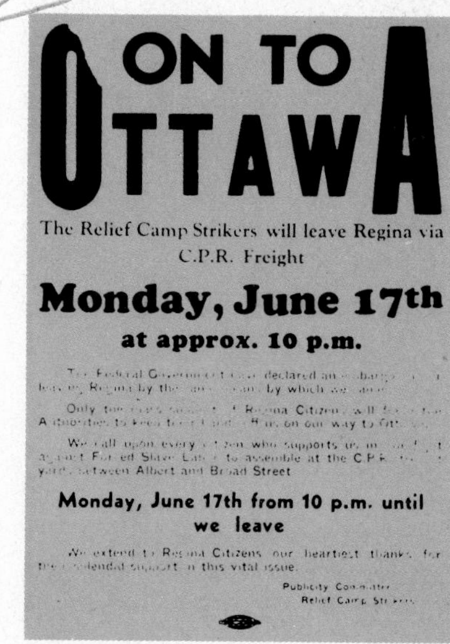

The On-To-Ottawa trekkers sat in Regina for two weeks while civic officials fumed and worried. Eight strikers, led by spokesman Arthur Evans, met with R.B. Bennett, but the PM dismissed the delegates and their petition as a subversive plot.

H.H. Stevens
Watchdog of Parliament Hill

One of Canada's most prominent, popular and feared men in the '30 s was Henry Herbert Stevens. Born in England in 1878, he moved with his family to B.C., and as a youth drove a stagecoach, prospected for gold and ran a weekly newspaper. As a young politician he single-handedly rid Vancouver of corrupt liquor interests and was elected to Commons in 1911. During the customs scandals of '26 he tore the lid off the can, bringing down the King government. A unique politician with scruples and deep social concern, he quit his post as Trade and Commerce minister after embarrassing the Bennett government with his 1934 probe into price spreads, but was returned to Ottawa the following year as the only elected member for his newly formed Reconstruction Party.

than ever before. Led by Robert Brodie, a small, Scottish-born veteran of the relief camps, the Regina riot and the RPWU, the unemployed were planning a massive strike that would bring the city to its knees. They decided to use the sheer weight of their presence to incapacitate three of the city's most important buildings – the Hotel Georgia, the Art Gallery and the Central Post Office.

New Deal for Canadians

The post office was the centre of activity. Sympathizers brought in cigarettes and food, and the men themselves organized musical events, races around the post office counters and innumerable singsongs. They even published a paper, *The Sitdowner's Gazette,* which was eagerly purchased by the public. Clergymen, union leaders and other sympathizers joined the strikers in their fun.

On Sunday, June 19, when the strike was thirty days old, the RCMP and local police arrived armed with tear gas bombs, and the good natured demonstration turned into a nasty, vicious fight. The men were clubbed and harassed by the police to such an extent that they and their supporters rioted through the downtown streets of Vancouver. Before the riots ended, forty people had been injured and twenty-one arrested. Property damage amounted to $39,000.

It was, however, the last great riot of the Great Depression. Although the Communist movement was stronger in the thirties than it had ever been, the actual number of its supporters was small. Most of those who joined the Party did so out of desperation rather than conviction, and most believed that the situation would ultimately come right.

Nonetheless, for the first time in Canada a large number of people began to consider drastic action to cure the ills of old-fashioned capitalism.

R.B. Bennett himself, epitome of conservatism, apostle of sound fiscal policies and devotee of balanced budgets, became what one conservative journalist described as a "crusading radical." Early in 1935 he went on the radio and astounded the public, and some conservative die-hards, with his proposals for a New Deal for the Canadian people. In the Speech from the Throne at the opening of his last session in 1935, he said:

You have been witnesses of grave defects and abuses in the capitalist system. Unemployment and want are proof of these. Great changes are taking place about us. New conditions prevail. These require modifications in the capitalist system to enable that system more effectively to serve the people.

During the session his government passed five key acts that would establish unemployment and social insurance, define minimum wages, set limitations on work hours and regulate marketing and the treatment of employees.

"It's King or Chaos"

R.B. Bennett's "conversion" to reform was too late to be taken very seriously (and to this day no one knows how sincere he was). After presiding over the worst five years of Depression the country had ever known, Bennett needed a miracle to gain re-election. In the 1935 campaign he even had to fight off attacks from his former Minister of Trade and Commerce, H.H. Stevens, who had resigned from the Cabinet and formed his own Reconstruction Party to demand still more reform in the interests of the little man. Not to mention threats from the CCF and Alberta's new Social Credit movement. With all of these new parties in the field in 1935, it looked as though the political system was about to follow the economy into collapse and no party would win enough seats to give the country stable government.

The Liberals, who had lain low in Opposition during the Bennett years, ran on the attractive slogan, "It's King or Chaos." Despite hardships and privation, Canadians were not ready for radical political change. In fact, they were frightened by it. The Liberals swept the country with 171 seats to the Conservatives' 39. The CCF took only 7 seats and Social Credit elected 17 (all in Alberta). Surprisingly, the Reconstruction Party got more votes nationally than the other new parties, but elected only one member, H.H. Stevens, and soon disappeared.

R.B. Bennett went off to England, was given a title, and died a few years later in semi-obscurity. His New Deal died too. Almost all of his 1935 legislation was thrown out by the courts as beyond the power of the federal government. In the last years of the decade the King government's main problem was how to overcome constitutional restraints on the federal government's ability to launch broad social welfare measures. Eventually, after years of negotiation and argument, the government of Canada followed the United States and Great Britain in building a welfare state and beginning to manage the economy according to the new economic theories of John Maynard Keynes.

All this came later, however. It would be at least another ten years before Canada was properly equipped to deal with the social problems that were encountered during the Great Depression.

Many small businesses went "belly up" in the early years of the Depression. With incomes cut or frozen and prices high, small-town merchants were forced to cut customers' credit. Large companies especially in the East suffered least, but their ads took on an austere new sales pitch.

Five Little Sweethearts

Annette, Emilie, Yvonne, Cécile and Marie – the world's first quintuplets to survive – arrived on May 28, 1934. Within days the five sisters were the sweethearts of the world. Their fight for survival was touch and go, but as soon as their lives were out of danger, contracts for commercial endorsements flooded in. Badly in need of money to clothe and feed his six older children and the new arrivals, Oliva Dionne followed the advice of the appointed guardians and took the show-biz route. All of a sudden, the Quints were everywhere, from decals on children's radios (right) to starring roles in the movies.

THE FIVE LITTLE SWEETHEARTS OF THE WORLD

Cecile Yvonne Marie Emilie Annette

The DIONNE QUINTUPLETS

THE DIONNE QUINTUPLETS
MAKE GOOD USE
OF THE OLD, OLD RHYMES
OF MOTHER GOOSE.

CECILE IS PLAYING
"LITTLE BO PEEP"
SHE'S HAPPY BECAUSE
SHE FOUND HER SHEEP.

"LITTLE MISS MUFFET"
IS YVONNE
HER CURDS AND WHEY
ARE NEARLY GONE.

"MARY CONTRARY"
YOU MAY KNOW
IS MARIE MAKING HER
GARDEN GROW.

EMILIE, HIDING HER
COAL BLACK HAIR,
PLAYS "GOLDILOCKS"
ALL PINK AND FAIR.

WHILE ANNETTE AS
"LITTLE RED RIDING HOOD"
SETS OUT FOR GRANDMOTHER'S
CARRYING FOOD.

"The Dionne Quintuplets make good use of the old, old rhymes of Mother Goose . . . " in this 1938 giveaway calendar.

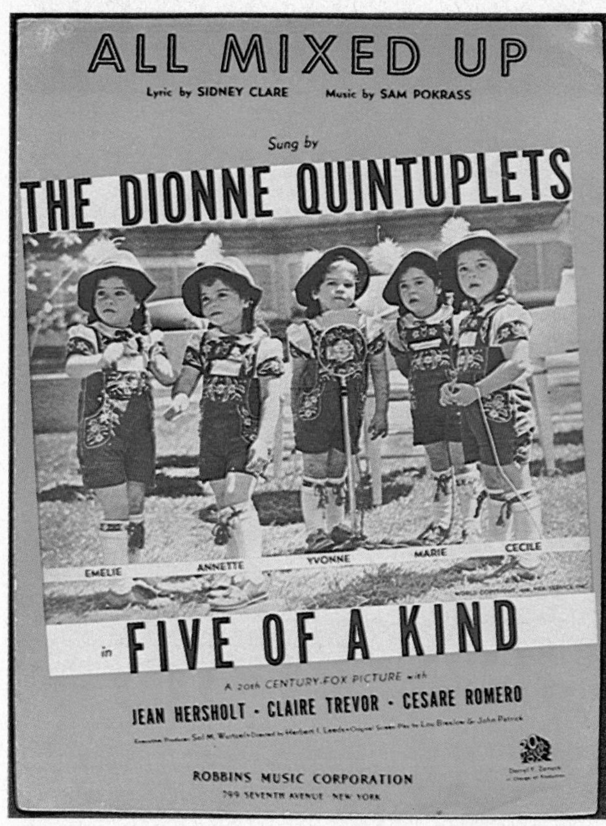

"All Mixed Up" in Five of a Kind *for 20th Century Fox, Hollywood, 1938: "Five little kiddies, All Mixed Up."*

A tin-plated paperweight – souvenir of Callander.

Karo

TO OUR FIRST LOVE

Karo

THE DIONNES

Karo is the only syrup served to the Dionne quintuplets. Its maltose and dextrose are ideal carbohydrates for growing children.

Allan Roy Dafoe, M.D.

One of a hundred ads that paid their way – a Valentine's Day promo for Karo Corn Syrup.

The DIONNE
QUINTUPLETS
We're Two Years Old
942
Copyright 1936 NEA Service

CHAPTER FOUR

The Million Dollar Babies

I have been chosen by God for a miracle.

Oliva Dionne, May 1934

Babies were important during the thirties. People who wanted them didn't dare have them. Couples who had them struggled to feed and clothe them. The marriage and birth rates declined during the decade, and birth control became a national controversy. Social workers and welfare agencies advocated it; clergymen denounced it. It is not surprising, therefore, that three of the most sensational news stories of the decade involved babies – having them, not having them and having too many of them.

Charles Vance Millar was a dignified Toronto lawyer, bulwark of the establishment, defender of the status quo, member of an inner circle of racehorse-owning sportsmen and one time winner of the King's Plate. When he was young, he had fallen in love with the beautiful daughter of a socially prominent Toronto family. His suit had been rejected because he was a $3-a-week lawyer who had not yet made his fortune. He never courted again; he never married and he had never been interested in children. When he died on October 31, 1926, he had left the bulk of his fortune to the Toronto woman who would within the next ten years produce the most children.

Although the "stork derby" clause of the Millar will got the most publicity, there were other, equally eccentric, clauses. To the former attorney-general of Ontario and the former head of the Methodist Church, both of whom had fought against horse racing and betting, Millar bequeathed each one share in the Ontario Jockey Club, worth $1,500. Each of the working ministers of the church in the communities of Walkerville, Sandwich and Windsor, received one share of the Kenilworth Jockey Club. Each practising Protestant minister in Toronto received one share of O'Keefe Brewing Company stock. His summer home in Jamaica went to three men who were bitter enemies. To people who had worked faithfully for him over the years Millar left little, and to his relatives he left nothing.

Breaking as it did all rules of propriety, the will was hotly contested. Everyone who did not get what they thought they should tried to break the will, including the Ontario Government which contended that the stork derby clause encouraged immorality. A learned judge, however, could not find that encouraging people to have children was in any way immoral. Ten years of legal manipulation could not break the will. Charlie Millar had been a good lawyer.

The stork derby provided newspaper headlines for ten years, keeping the curious titillated and the population entertained. For ten years, weary re-

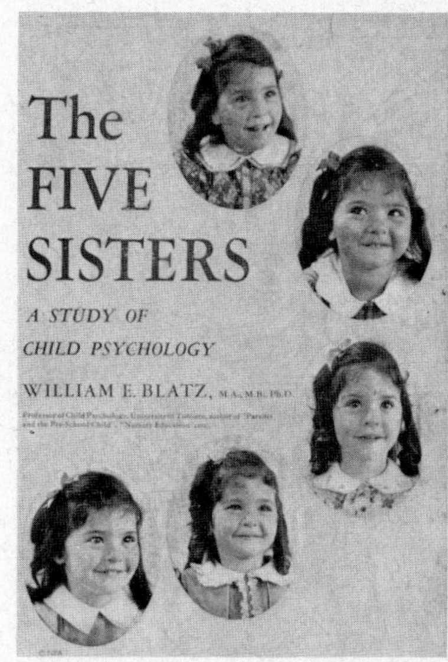

Although popular psychology had made its debut in Canada in the twenties, Dr. William Blatz created a minor furore among parents with this book.

Opposite page: *While the birth rate dropped 3.6% from 1930 to 1940, the Dionne quintuplets dominated world headlines and the attention of all.*

Dorothea Palmer
A Subject of Controversy

On Sept. 13, 1936, an Ottawa woman was arrested by police in the small French-speaking town of Eastview, Ont. Charged under Section 207 of the Criminal Code for "unlawfully advertising and selling contraceptive drugs and devices," Dorothea Palmer, a 28-year-old, Welsh-born bookstore clerk, made one long-distance phone call and with it launched one of the most unusual trials in Canadian history. Her employer, A.R. Kaufman, a Kitchener rubber goods producer who operated under the cover of the Parents' Information Bureau, lined up two of the best defence lawyers in the country. The trial lasted six months and 750,000 words of testimony were transcribed from expert witnesses. When it was all over, Dorothea Palmer was a free woman and Canadian parents had the right to make decisions regarding their private lives and families.

porters poked around in overcrowded tenements, talking to harassed mothers and weary husbands. The derby caused misery to hundreds of mothers who competed for the prize and lost, because to have one child less than the winner was to have, in most cases, a family that was a great burden to support.

$12,500 for her troubles

At one point a plucky young matron by the name of Mae Clark claimed the prize on the grounds that she had produced ten children within the stipulated period. Investigation revealed that she had ten, all right, but only five of them were by her legal husband. The paternity of the other five was doubtful. This situation precipitated a legal battle to determine whether illegitimate births could qualify for the jackpot. Millar had not stipulated, saying only that the money would go to the Toronto mother having the greatest number of children "as shown under the Vital Statistics Act." The court righteously decided that Mae Clark's illegitimate offspring didn't count.

When the ten years finally came to an end, four Toronto women tied for the prize. Each had produced nine children and each received $165,000. All of the women were in modest circumstances; one of them had been on relief. Even Mae Clark got $12,500 for her troubles, voted by the winners to prevent lengthy legal suits.

No one will ever know what possessed Charles Millar to draw up a will that he knew would offend many of his business associates, most of those who had ever worked for him, all of his relatives and, directly or indirectly, every clergyman in the province, regardless of denomination. We do know that he was dead set against the government ban on birth control. Had he been alive, therefore, on October 21, 1936, just ten days before his stork derby would reward willful fecundity on four counts, he might have been amused by proceedings in a small magistrate's court in Eastview, Ontario. Dorothea Palmer was paraded before the court and charged under Section 207 of the Criminal Code with calling on the women of Eastview, a predominantly French-Canadian suburb of Ottawa, and giving them advice on how to limit and space the number of their offspring. For this heinous crime, the formidable forces of the Crown were ranged against her, determined to prove her guilty and, possibly, to send her to jail.

She had been picked up while leaving the house of one of her "victims" and held in custody pending bail of $500. Since she was only a clerk in a small Ottawa bookstore and apparently without friends or influence, her situation looked bleak.

She was permitted one phone call, however, and the result of that call brought immediate assistance from her other employer, Mr. A.R. Kaufman of Kitchener, who brought with him two of the ablest criminal lawyers in the province. Thus was the stage set for one of the longest, most expensive and famous trials in Canadian history.

free birth control information

A manufacturer of rubber goods, Mr. Kaufman was also the organizer and manager of the Parents' Information Bureau, whose purpose was to inform and educate women on the ways to plan their children. Miss Palmer functioned as a part-time social worker who called on housewives, giving them free birth control information. The prosecution, of course, questioned Mr. Kaufman's motives. Did he not manufacture contraceptives? Section 207 was quite specific on the point that selling or advertising contraceptive drugs or devices was a crime, but a subsection stated that no persons could be convicted if they could prove they acted in the public good. Kaufman's high priced lawyers based their defence on the proposition that he and his employee were acting in the public good. This, then, became the nub of the argument: were contraceptives good for society or not?

The chief witness for the prosecution was a medical doctor who stated that in his opinion the use of contraceptives without a doctor's advice was wrong but hedged considerably when asked under cross examination if he thought that the non-use of contraceptives could sometimes be harmful. He finally admitted that this was so and also that the rhythm method, as advocated by the Catholic Church, was not infallible. He was also appalled at the number of illegal abortions and concerned over the health of some mothers who kept on having children regardless of their health or financial circumstances.

nine children and $3 a week

The defence lawyers brought to the witness stand an array of psychologists (including the noted Brock Chisholm), relief inspectors, doctors, professors, social workers, preachers and experts on birth control. Miss Anna Weber, head nurse at the Parents' Information Bureau, testified that most doctors did not know much about birth control, so women could get little help from their doctor.

The defence quoted from the books of the most reputable people in the field, including the noted English author Marie Stopes, one of the world's most prominent crusaders for birth control. The problem of the public cost of uncontrolled family size was demonstrated by one couple who had nine children and an income of $3 a week, and by a woman who was raising twelve children on relief. The courtroom was packed with Ottawa housewives, who had a certain stake in the proceedings.

The Crown could not prove that the defendant or her employer were making any money from the service. As a matter of fact, their devices sold for

Bringing up baby in the 1930s. Mothers who could, still nursed; other warmed up glass bottles. Home remedies such as "gripe water" were common and visits from the doctor rare.

Family Business

Babies, weddings and matters of the home took on new importance in the thirties. The family had to survive, and everyone from the parish priest to the Hollywood film maker turned the public concern into news. Girls across North America turned into Shirley Temple doubles; contests of all sorts focused on baby; and ads used babies to sell almost anything.

America's sweetheart visits the Empress Hotel in Victoria, B.C.

Winnipeg's "Treasure Trail" radio show challenges local daddies to an on-the-air baby diapering contest.

Over a thousand spectators fill DeLorimier Stadium in Montreal as 105 couples are married by 104 priests in this single ceremony in 1939.

considerably less than the prices charged in drugstores all over the country, where contraceptives were sold openly and without prosecution. Despite all this, Magistrate Lester H. Clayton took one whole month before ruling that the defendant was indeed working for the public good.

If Elzire Dionne had lived in Toronto, she would have won the stork derby by several lengths. She would probably have wrapped it up on May 28, 1934 when, already the mother of six, she gave birth to five girls in Callander, Ontario. The Dionne Quintuplets became a bigger tourist attraction than Niagara Falls. Doctors, midwives, nurses, politicians, psychologists, photographers and writers rode to fame on the ties of their dainty pinafores. There was more ballyhoo, hokum, promotion, and wild rumour connected with them than with any children ever born into this world.

Despite all this, these five charming, smiling, patty-caking little tykes were far and away the nicest thing that happened in the thirties. Canadians soon knew more about Annette, Cécile, Emilie, Yvonne and Marie than they did about their own children.

true-north-strong-and-free

They were born into a family as poor as many others in the thirties, and that made things easier for millions. They gave Canada a world record – the chances of quintuplets being born were one in 57 million, and no quints in the history of the world had ever survived for more than a few minutes. There was something so true-north-strong-and-free about them, and Canadian hearts swelled with pride as though they had done it themselves. The Yankees had Hollywood and Shirley Temple and the Empire State Building, but by God they didn't have the Quints!

When Dr. Allan Roy Dafoe arrived at the tiny Dionne farmhouse shortly after four on the morning of May 28, an aunt, Donalda Legros, and a midwife, Madame Benoit Lebel, had already delivered two tiny, bluish, premature babies, and a third was on the way. He delivered the new arrival and placed it beside the other two who were emitting weak little cries like the mewing of kittens. Before he could do more than mop the mother's brow, however, two more babies arrived almost together. After attending to the babies and the mother, he drove off in his car to fetch the parish priest. Dr. Dafoe had been practising medicine in the Callander district for twenty-seven years and he was sure that before dawn some or all of his patients would require holy unction.

popped into a butcher's basket

When the doctor returned everybody was still alive. Mrs. Dionne had improved remarkably and was breathing freely and asking about her babies. When told there were five of them she wearily shook her head back and forth on the pillow and wondered aloud how they would ever feed and clothe so many children. The father, Oliva Dionne, was quoted as saying he was the kind of guy who should be put in jail.

Because the babies had arrived two months early no preparations had been made for one, let alone five. In other circumstances, the tiny mites would have been popped into an incubator with controlled temperature and humidity and regular doses of oxygen to keep them breathing. Instead, they were popped into a butcher's basket that Auntie Legros had fetched from her home across the road, wrapped in squares of wool torn from a blanket and warmed with heated flatirons placed against the outside of the basket.

Somehow they kept on breathing, and the country doctor felt as long as there was breath there was hope. He gave the weary attendants instructions to keep the babies warm and give

The Nugget — LATE EDITION

QUINTUPLETS BORN TO FARM WIFE

French Fliers at Brooklyn Field Land Safely After Ocean Flight Today

Two Bush Fires Sweeping Over Sudbury Area

World Nations Turn to Russia To Avert War

LATE WIRE FLASHES

24-Year Old Corbeil Mother Establishes Canadian Mark

$200,000 DAMAGE IN ROUYN REGION

POLICE AT SPRAGGE NAB ROBBERS QUICK

More Good Wishes For Young Mother

SUSPECT FOUL PLAY IN BELLEVILLE DEATH

Stove Explodes Suspect Revenge

Corbeil Eclipses Maritime Record

FOUR MEN ATTEMPT LIFE OF AMBASSADOR TO CUBA

COLOMBO STILL FAVORED AS TURF CLASSIC NEARS

The North Bay Nugget, *May 28, 1934: the first newspaper to get the story. As soon as the item hit the Canadian Press wire, the news was on the air and on the front page near and far.*

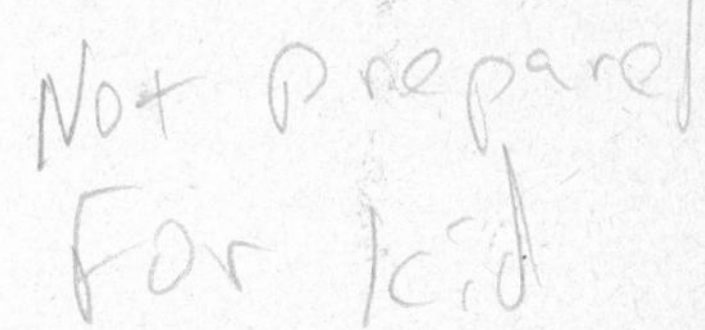

them a few drops of warm water every two hours. He attended to the mother carefully and went home for some much needed sleep. On the street of Callander he told some people that he had just delivered five babies to Elzire Dionne but didn't think it was worth phoning the editor of the North Bay *Nugget* to tell him. The *Nugget* was informed eventually by an uncle of the babies, Leon Dionne, and the editor sent the details out on the Canadian Press wire. In no time the news went around the globe, and the outside world began to move in on the Quints.

The first to come were a photographer and reporter from the *Nugget*. They persuaded Madame Legros to remove the new babies from their warm nest and put them into bed with their mother for a nice human interest picture. Then they got a picture of the proud father holding the basket full of babies. Right after they left, a reporter from the Toronto *Star* appeared, notebook in hand. When the parents could not tell him how much the babies weighed, he obligingly offered to help weigh them. The total weight, according to an old potato scale resurrected from the back shed, was thirteen pounds, six ounces.

North American advertisers picked up the Quints' story in various ways. Toothpaste, corn syrup, soap and baby products producers used direct endorsement to sell their lines, while Life Savers used the magic number to sell their five-flavour package.

long distance call from Chicago

When Dr. Dafoe returned, he was furious to learn what was going on and gave orders that the babies were not to be disturbed. The new nurse he brought with him took care of that.

The next impingement from the outside world was a pre-dawn, long distance call to Dr. Dafoe from the president of the Chicago Board of Health, who was an expert on premature babies and wildly excited about the prospects of the quintuplets living. For a half hour he talked to the little country doctor explaining his views, giving advice and filling Dafoe with hope for the lives of the now-famous five.

The fight to save the babies continued. Farmers coming in from the dry, dusty fields in Saskatchewan asked first about the Quints. Fishermen on the east coast and men in the far north, getting their news over the newly formed Canadian Radio Broadcasting Commission, forgot their own troubles while waiting for the latest bulletin.

They heard that the doctor had given each a few drops of greatly diluted rum and they wondered if that wouldn't kill the tykes. The public heard that there was a need for breast milk, and nursing mothers wished they were close enough to give some of their own. When Sunday came, preachers throughout the nation added special prayers for the "miracle babies sent by God to these humble people." School children talked about little else. Hitler, Mussolini and the war in China were all crowded out of mind by the thought of five tiny babies fighting for their lives.

"Father has offer of $50,000 . . . "

Headline followed headline: "Quints amaze medical world." "Quints' parents eligible for King's Bounty of three pounds sterling." And then came the one that shocked everyone: "Father has offer of $50,000 to take kids to the Chicago World's Fair."

Desperate for money to support his family of eleven, Oliva Dionne had actually signed a contract. But he had been very careful about it, consulting his parish priest and, most important, insisting on a clause saying that the babies could not be moved without the consent of the doctor. The children did not travel to Chicago.

The five lived on, each day setting a new record for longevity of quintuplets. Nurse Louise de Kiriline, who had worked with Dr. Dafoe on many occasions, moved into the tiny farmhouse and, under the doctor's direction, instituted a strict regimen of sanitation and non-interference. She ordered the place scrubbed and scoured, put up screens to keep out the flies, and laid down an edict that everything, including the diapers, should be boiled, and everybody, including the parents, should keep away from the babies until they were out of danger.

By now help was coming from all sides. Breast milk arrived from the Hospital for Sick Children in Toronto, the Royal Victoria Hospital in Montreal and even from Chicago. The Red Cross was hard on the job and incubators arrived. Gifts of materials and money poured in from all sides and a special emergency committee was appointed to look after the donations.

The problem of crowded quarters and chaotic conditions persisted. It became evident that if the quintuplets were to have any chance to survive they would have to be protected from disease, promoters, kidnappers, their adoring fans, and even, some people felt, from their parents. It was obvious that they needed special quarters of their own, and the Red Cross decided to build a hospital across the road from the Dionne farm.

"I found a million dollar baby"

The new hospital was equipped with the best and most modern of everything. It was laid out so that the children would have the ultimate in sunlight, fresh air and spotless accommodation – everything that children could possibly want, except a mother. She was permitted to visit at specified times but she had no voice in how they should be cared for.

One popular song of the day exclaimed: "I found a million dollar baby in a five and ten cent store." The Ontario Government realized that they'd found five million dollar babies in the northern bush. They took it for granted that they knew what was best for the girls, just as they certainly knew what was best for Ontario. In 1935,

The curious came by the thousands – as many as 6,000 in one day. Here a gaggle of early-birds waits outside the midwives' souvenir shop. Tourists spent an estimated $51 million in 1934.

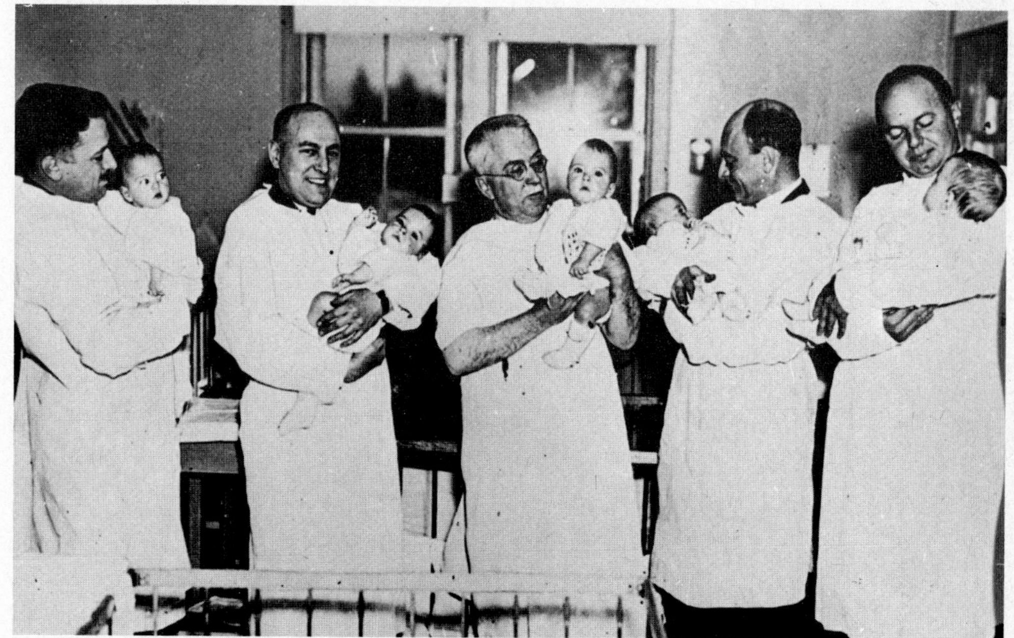

The babies need no introduction, but that's Dr. Dafoe (centre), Premier Mitch Hepburn (far right), and David Croll (far left). Ontario assumed custody of the Quints in '35.

Dr. William Blatz
The Quints' Counsellor

The man behind the one-way glass at the Dionne Quints' home was Dr. William Blatz, Canada's top child psychologist. Born in Hamilton in 1895, the youngest of nine children, he was educated at the Universities of Toronto and Chicago. One of his first studies was of the effects of combat on WW I soldiers. In 1926, backed by a Rockefeller grant, he established the Toronto Institute of Child Study, the world's first nursery for the study of pre-school children. When public concern was raised about the abnormal, fish-bowl environment of the Quints, Blatz was the obvious choice for the job of advisor. It was a minor claim to fame. Author of the international bestseller, *Understanding the Young Child* (1944), and five other books, he is best known for his sensible theories, lectures and work with parents, teachers and children.

the Hepburn government passed the Dionne Quintuplet Act, which took the children away from their parents and made them wards of the province. A board of guardians was appointed and given power over the childrens' lives and finances. Oliva Dionne was a member of the board, but he was always outvoted. The government proceeded to build the Quints into a sideshow.

The government called in as a consultant the most famous baby-raising expert of the day, Dr. William E. Blatz of the Toronto Institute of Child Study. Blatz and his staff organized the children's activities, observed them, tested them, weighed them, planned their play, their rest periods, their elimination routines, dining-room routines, and how they were disciplined. It was Blatz who instituted the "silent room" in which a child could be shut away from her sisters as a "consequence" of unsocial behaviour. But they were never spanked. It was a marvellous opportunity for science to work a controlled experiment with five almost identical specimens. How good it was for the five little ones would be another story.

6,000 in one day

To prepare for the tourists, the government built a good road from Highway 11 to the hospital, put two high fences around the property, and posted two provincial police on round-the-clock surveillance.

They came by the millions, as many as 6,000 in one day at the peak. They lined up in the sun or cold or rain waiting for the 11:00 AM and 3:00 PM shows. They saw a cute baby held up by a nurse who also held up a sign reading Annette, or Yvonne, or Cécile, or Emilie, or Marie. Marie was the smallest and had had the hardest struggle to survive, and for that reason she was the favourite. Most of the viewers were too far away to see the babies clearly, but when one of the tots would laugh or smile or clap her hands, those closest would break into delighted laughter and the ones further back would follow suit.

Later, when the children could walk and ride tricycles and climb jungle gyms, a special walkway was constructed so that the tourists could file through and watch the children at play. A special screen allowed visitors to see the children but prevented the children from seeing the visitors. This show was a source of great delight to the visitors, and some came back time and again to watch it.

"fertility stones"

After seeing the Quints, the crowd thronged into the souvenir shops. In one of these the two midwives, Madame Legros and Madame Lebel, sold post cards, pictures, pennants, blotters, whisks, story books, and a host of other items, including a 25-cent booklet in which they told their own story of the fateful night of May 28.

Also on display was the actual butcher's basket into which the tiny arrivals had first been placed. It was not for sale, of course, but people gazed at it in wonder as it hung from the rafters. For an extra 50 cents visitors could stand on the flat roof of the pavilion and view the hospital and the show through a pair of binoculars.

Other booths sold a variety of refreshments. Eager parents, perhaps hopeful of emulating the Dionnes, could even buy "fertility stones" picked up on the Dionne farm, or when that supply was gone, trucked in from gravel pits. And across the road the visitors could see the little farm house where the famous five had been born and where Oliva and Elzire lived with the rest of the children.

Beyond the house they could see parts of the rocky, bush-covered 300-acre farm from which Oliva Dionne had managed to scrape a living before fame and fortune hit. Some visitors even knocked on the door to buy tinted photographs of the famous five that were sold by the parents.

Of all the people making money from the Quints, the parents were making the least. Nearly everybody else, except Dr. Dafoe who received nothing more than his fees, was making a bundle. Callander, a worn-out lumber town, prospered. Hotels, motels, and restaurants had customers lined up waiting to get in. The filling station in Callander named the five gas pumps after the children and customers would gleefully shout, "Fill her up with Cécile." Real estate values soared. Many of the farmers around took in overnight guests. The money spent by tourists on their way to Callander was estimated in 1934 at $51 million. Two years later it had doubled. The Quints were the biggest tourist attraction Ontario had ever had.

The Quints themselves made money, too. Besides the fee for exclusive picture rights, the guardians signed contracts for endorsement of canned milk, syrup, dolls, baby clothes, soap, breakfast foods, baby foods. There were movie contracts, including $50,000 from 20th-Century Fox for "The Country Doctor," starring the Quints and actor Jean Hersholt, and others for even greater amounts. From all sources, their earnings were estimated at well over $1 million.

Meanwhile, the conflict between the parents and the guardians had been building. Oliva and Elzire Dionne steadfastly believed that children are better off with their parents. The end of the decade practically saw the end of the Quints as public property. Through court action, the parents won control of their children and the Quints rejoined their family. Later, Oliva designed and built a huge house near the nursery and the entire family moved in. Most of the people who remember the Quints do so with gratitude for the excitement, affection, and wonder that they brought into their lives, at a time when those commodities were most needed.

Jokebook

Every generation has its own sense of humour. Canadians in the '30s laughed at Knock-knock jokes, Confucius say . . . , Little Audrey jokes, handies (ten-finger hand mimes), Mae West jokes, and almost anything else that could get a grin. In tight money days, they might pop a "Hoople cheque" in the mail for a friend.

"One million and one—one million and two—one million and three."

"As one broker to another—Brother, can you spare a dime?"

This country needs the courage to spend its cash, states one of these business economists. All right mister, if you'll put up the cash, we'll put up the courage.

Toronto *Globe*

The candidate who keeps his ear to the ground while sitting on the fence is doing a remarkable acrobatic feat–to say nothing of talking through his hat at the same time, especially after he's thrown his hat into the ring.

Port Arthur *News-Chronicle*

It is reported that among the paper currency to be issued by the Bank of Canada may be $2.50 bills. If so, they will be a distinct novelty.

Portage la Prairie *Graphic*

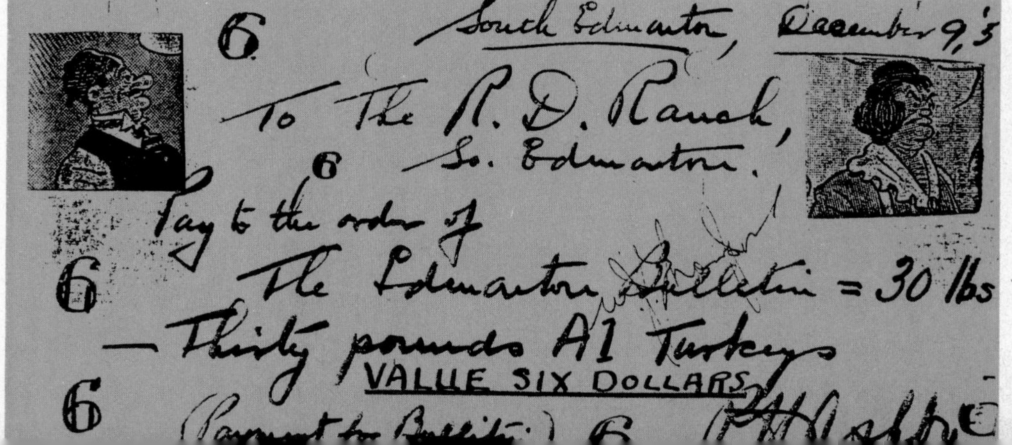

6 South Edmonton, December 9,

To The R. D. Ranch,
So. Edmonton.

Pay to the order of
The Edmonton Bulletin = 30 lbs
— Thirty pounds A1 Turkeys
VALUE SIX DOLLARS
(Payment for Bulletin)

Although air connections with the Arctic were established in the late '20s, northern outposts continued to rely on basic ground transport to bring home supplies and the mail. This Bellanca airbus is unloading at Cameron Bay at Great Bear Lake.

CHAPTER FIVE

Northern Flights

... a series of breath-taking excursions into the north by a new breed of coureurs de bois *... "bush pilots."*

Pierre Berton in *The Mysterious North*

Interest in flying was at an intense peak in the thirties. In 1930, over a million people had come to stare at the great British dirigible, *R-100,* which had flown from Cardington, England, to Montreal in 78 hours and 52 minutes, with fifty-five people aboard. Three years before, in 1927, the Department of National Defence had agreed to provide two aircraft to any organization that would train pilots, and to pay $100 a head for each man trained. Flying clubs in operation at the time took advantage of the offer, and other clubs quickly organized in cities from coast to coast. By the beginning of the decade, there were over twenty such clubs with thousands of members, and the Canadian Flying Club Association was formed.

In 1931 the Association staged the first of its annual air pageants in Hamilton, Ontario. Crack private pilots along with those of the RCAF had the audiences gasping. Thousands of cars jammed the highways to the airport and parked around the landing strips. The pilots went up in the latest planes, looped the loop, did barrel rolls, roared in low over the parked cars and did formation flying. There was often a parachute jump to take the breath away.

After the show there was always a lineup of young men bitten by the flying bug, anxious to join up for lessons. Women also took to the air and became accomplished fliers. Daphne Paterson of Saint John qualified for her commercial pilot's licence in 1930. Nellie Carson of Saskatoon established an altitude record for women that same year, flying at 16,000 feet, out of sight and hearing of the spectators on the ground. Kamloop's Jeanne Gilbert was the most travelled airwoman in Canada before World War II.

The adventures of the bush pilots were a natural extension of the stunting and barnstorming of the twenties. Most of the bush pilots had gotten flying in their blood during World War I and never managed to get it out. Even their names suggest daring – "Doc" Oaks and "Wop" May, "Punch" Dickins and J.H. Tudhope, Grant McConachie and Walter Gilbert.

"Wop" May and Vic Horner had braved below-zero temperatures in an open cockpit to fly life-saving serum to diphtheria-stricken Fort Vermilion; "Punch" Dickins had made the first aerial crossing of the Arctic Circle in central Canada; Fred McCall had flown 300 quarts of nitro-glycerine into Calgary where it was urgently needed in the Turner Valley oil field; Conway Farrell had made so many Arctic flights he was known as the Santa Claus of the North. They were strong, resourceful, extraordinarily adaptable and often

Formed in 1930, James Richardson's Canadian Airways was one of the first companies operating regular survey and exploration flights to the ore deposits of the north.

C. H. "Punch" Dickins
The Man Who Opened The Arctic

In the days when Edmonton, Calgary and Winnipeg were among the busiest flight centres of North America, a young pilot named "Punch" Dickins was putting the Arctic on the map. Born in Edmonton, he received his licence at a time when flying was still a reckless adventure. In the last years of the 1920s, a time of exhaustive exploration in the North, he flew the first aerial survey of the Barrens with the McAlpine party, a distance of almost 4,000 miles. In '29 he was the first flyer to reach the western Arctic, carrying mail to Aklavik and furs back to Edmonton. By 1930 he had logged more miles in the North than any other pilot, and it was largely through his pioneer efforts that the uncharted regions of the Yukon and the NWT became an essential part of the country.

extremely lucky. And the site of their greatest daring was Edmonton, Alberta.

Furthest north of all Canadian cities, Edmonton has always been a centre of exploration and northern travel. Settlements had been established north from Edmonton all the way to the Arctic Ocean. For centuries, reaching them had been a long and tortuous journey. The bush pilots outfitted their old war planes with pontoons or skis and made the same journey in a matter of hours. The city of Edmonton became the busiest, wackiest, most exciting air centre in the world – the "gateway to the north," a "crossroads of the world."

meant almost certain death

When gold and silver had been discovered in the precambrian rock north of Edmonton, the air traffic increased enormously. A steady stream of aircraft carried prospectors, engineers, food, supplies and equipment, everybody and everything that needed to get into the north. In 1929 more than 445 planes were registered in Canada, carrying 125,000 passengers and 4 million pounds of freight. Most of this activity was out of Edmonton. By 1935, Edmonton's total air freight amounted to 26 million pounds, which was more than the total air freight carried by Great Britain, the United States, France and Germany combined.

Much of this flying was done during the worst weather conditions possible, in aircraft that had few of the navigational aids we have today. The bitter cold of the Arctic frosted over windows so that the pilots could not see, and in planes that were to sit on the ground overnight the cold could turn the engine oil into a solid black block. The oil had to be drained each night. Sudden blizzards completely hid the ground within minutes and blew light planes far off their course. A forced landing in winter, hundreds of miles from any settlement, meant almost certain death.

In early October of 1930, pilot Paddy Burke and his engineer Emil Kading were flying a prospector named Robert Martin from Lower Post on the Liard River across the mountains to the little fur-trading and mining settlement of Atlin on Atlin Lake. A sudden blizzard came upon them and with great luck Burke was able to bring the plane down on the Liard River. River stones had ripped their pontoons beyond repair. They had no radio, very little food, one winter sleeping bag and several lighter ones, a rifle and twelve rounds of ammunition, and the snow was falling fast.

A rescue plane was sent out when they did not reach Atlin, but could see nothing at all on the ground and was forced to give up the search temporarily. Another rescue plane ran into fog and nose-dived into the sea with no survivors. Finally pilot Everett Wasson, along with his guide Joe Walsh, took off in a blizzard, determined to search until he found his lost friends.

the redoubtable Wasson

Often throughout the long weeks that followed, Wasson had to land his plane on the ice of the twisting Liard River where a tiny miscalculation would have hurled him into the bush and rock along the bank. Before he could take off from the river, he and Walsh had to tramp the deep snow back and forth with snowshoes to make a base hard enough for the plane to achieve take-off speed. On one occasion, the redoubtable Wasson actually ran on his snowshoes along beside the open door of the cockpit until he gathered enough speed. Then, snowshoes dangling, he hauled himself up into the cabin.

Finally after almost two months Walsh's practiced eyes spotted a shadow on the snow of the Liard River. It was the Junkers aircraft that the three men had abandoned. Wasson landed on a small lake fifteen miles away and the two men

Flights to the Arctic

These were the days when pilots bundled up and flew "by the seat of their pants." Scores of daring, history-making flights were made, each one riddled with problems – bad weather, mechanical failures or the uncharted nature of the territories. Whether the purpose was scientific, commercial or medical, the vast, unknown barrens became the landing strip for dozens of pilots whose names and accomplishments are legendary.

Bush pilots without equal, "Wop" May and Vic Horner, who flew serum to frozen Fort Vermilion during an epidemic.

In 1930 Walter Gilbert flew the North Magnetic Pole exploration crew into the Arctic: (l to r) Stan Knight, Richard Finnie, Gilbert and Major Burwash.

snowshoed to the stranded plane, where they found a note telling them the lost men had gone upstream in search of food.

Knowing where they had gone and finding them were two different things, however. First they had to fly back to Whitehorse to refuel and get supplies. Here, after studying charts, it was decided to head for the Pelly Indian Reserve. Over the Pelly Mountain Range, Walsh spotted a thin wisp of smoke curling up above the trees. Making a low run over the spot, they saw two floundering, exhausted men.

The Curious Case of Grey Owl

WITH US AGAIN WITH WONDERFUL FILMS!

After a brilliant and overwhelmingly successful tour of The British Isles and the United States and A Command Performance at Buckingham Palace

GREY OWL

WILL SHOW HIS PICTURES AND TALK ON

"BACK TO MY BEAVER PEOPLE"

— AT —

MASSEY HALL, SATURDAY, MARCH 26th

Commencing 8 p.m. sharp. Doors open 7.30.

RESERVE YOUR SEATS EARLY AND BRING YOUR FRIENDS!

Tickets: $1.00 and 50c.

Remember! If you want your seats in blocks book early!
Tickets may be secured by telephoning Mr. Eric Gaskell, RA. 2867, or Mrs. King, HU. 1441.

THE STUDENT'S IMPRESSION OF GREY OWL!

The Toronto Branch of The Canadian Authors' Association offers two prizes for the best essays by any high or secondary school student on the theme of Grey Owl's appearance and remarks while on the Massey Hall platform on the evening of March 26th.

FIRST PRIZE!

ANY TWO OF GREY OWL'S BOOKS (AUTOGRAPHED)

"Tales of an Empty Cabin" "Sajo and Her Beaver People" "Pilgrims of the Wild" "Men of the Last Frontier" "The Tree"

SECOND PRIZE!

ANY ONE OF THE FIVE

Preferred length 300 words. Limit 500 words. Entries to reach Mr. Eric Gaskell, 40 Nanton Ave., Toronto, by April 9th. Presentations will be made at the Canadian Authors' Association Annual Dinner May 14th.

UNDER THE AUSPICES OF THE TORONTO BRANCH OF THE CANADIAN AUTHOR'S ASSOCIATION

Archie Belaney, alias "Grey Owl"– the magnificent fraud of the '30s.

Born and raised in England, he covered up his past, became a "native," and lived in the bush.

Totally steeped in the ways of the wild, he was an expert marksman, trapper and scout for hunting and fishing parties. His wife, Anahareo (centre), actually was a native.

Kading's last two rifle shells

The rescue, however, had just begun. First, boxes of food were dumped out of the aircraft cabin to land as close to the men as possible. Wasson located a lake about a dozen miles away on which he could make a landing. From there it was a long hike on snowshoes through the bush to the stranded men. Having dropped all their food, they had to find them or perish themselves.

When the early darkness hit, Wasson and Walsh were forced to stop for the night. At first light they started out again, but realized to their horror that they had missed the spot where they had dropped the food. Carefully they backtracked, took what bearings they could and began the search again. Nothing. Then, as they shouted desperately into the vast emptiness, they heard the far-off crack of a rifle. Another. Following the sound, they came upon the men. Kading and Martin had gotten the food boxes and were having their first good meal in weeks. The pilot, Paddy Burke, had died just two weeks before. Sweat formed under Walsh's toque when he learned that the shots they heard were made by Kading's last two rifle shells.

The most legendary bush pilot was Wilfred Reid "Wop" May. A war ace with thirteen confirmed victories, it was May who was being chased by the legendary Red Baron, Manfred von Richthofen, when Canadian Roy Brown got on the German ace's tail and shot him down. May had flown thousands of miles over the northland delivering everything from cows and husky dogs to canoes and fur. It was May who answered an RCMP call for assistance in the winter of 1932 to hunt the "mad trapper of Rat River."

15-hour gun battle

The RCMP had received complaints from the Indians along Rat River that someone was robbing their traps. Albert Johnson was the suspect. Johnson shot the Mountie who came to his cabin to investigate and disappeared from his cabin after a 15-hour gun battle. He eluded the Mounties over 600 miles of Arctic terrain, zigzagging craftily toward the mountains, backtracking and mingling his tracks with those of the caribou herds.

Wop May answered the Mounties call, in a Bellanca monoplane carrying dynamite, tear gas, ammunition and supplies for the beleaguered search party. From the air, May could observe Johnson's movements. He knew Johnson was backtracking and could see where Johnson and the posse would eventually confront each other. May reported all this information to those waiting on the ground.

Johnson was brought down in a barrage of gunfire but managed to wound one Mountie. May saved the life of the wounded policeman by rushing him to the hospital in Aklavik and later he brought out the rest of the posse in a series of flights. Albert Johnson had led the Mounties on a gruelling 29-day chase and killed two of their officers in one of the most spectacular manhunts in the history of this country.

At first, bush pilots flew at random – going where they were needed whenever they were

The Search for the Mad Trapper

One of the most sensational manhunts in history began at this cabin on Rat River. Here Albert Johnson shot and killed a Mountie. He escaped and the search was on.

"Wop" May (left) standing beside the single-engine Bellanca in which he tracked Johnson from the air.

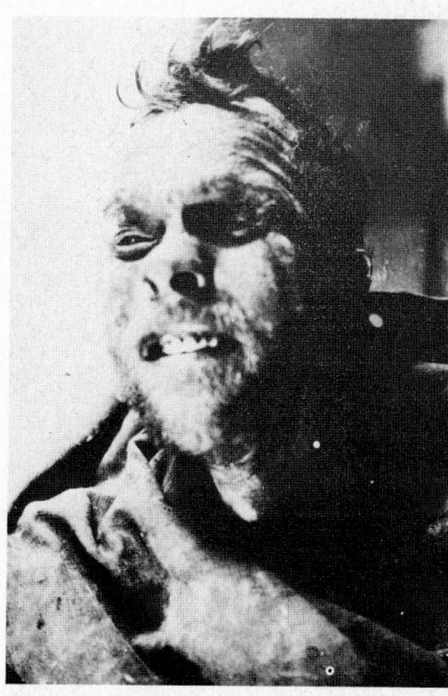

The only extant photo of Johnson, shot down after a 29-day chase.

needed. As their numbers and their flights increased, it became obvious that regularly scheduled flights to carry mail and parcels and passengers could be supported. Gradually the air mail routes had become more regular, the federal government had issued more official mail contracts and individual bush pilots had increased their equipment and consolidated their routes. In 1931, an amalgamation of several of these individual companies resulted in Canadian Airways which ran a first-rate air-mail service.

Still, commercial flight lagged behind in Canada until April 10, 1937, when an act of Parliament created the publicly-owned Trans-Canada Air Lines. The new airline possessed two Lockheed 10-passenger airplanes and one Boeing biplane which was used for mail and for surveying new routes. For two years the new airline made experimental flights. By 1939, the airline had accumulated fifteen 10-passenger Lockheeds and 497 employees. On April 1, 1939, TCA's first passenger flight took off from Vancouver enroute to Montreal. The plane was a twin-engined Lockheed 10A, which carried ten passengers and flew at the amazing speed of 220 miles per hour. The interior consisted of two rows of five seats, with a narrow aisle between, up and down which a stewardess wended her precarious way with food, non-alcoholic beverages, pillows, aspirin and tender loving care. One reporter compared the sensation of flying to relaxing in your favourite chair with the maid using a vacuum cleaner in a nearby room, and "there you have it, engine noise and all."

It was not an express flight, of course. Stops were necessary at Lethbridge, Winnipeg, Kapuskasing and North Bay for fuel and supplies. At each stop passengers could catch connecting planes to other centres along the way.

The pilot flew along the route of a radio beam. There were meteorological stations, weather men and air controllers all along the route. The total time of the trip, including stops, was fifteen hours. A similar trip by train would have taken three days and four nights. The one way fare, Vancouver to Montreal, including meals was $130.90, or six cents per mile, with a 10 per cent discount for purchasing a round trip ticket. Toronto passengers changed planes at North Bay and were in Malton an hour later.

It was the start. Not even the gruelling Depression which had broken some people's spirits and others' fortunes could keep in rein the vision of a group of daring young men who parlayed a thirst for adventure into a multi-billion dollar industry.

When TCA began commercial service in 1937, passengers on the 122-mile flight from Vancouver to Seattle could enjoy the luxury in ten-seat Lockheed Electras similar to this.

Port Out; Starboard Home

"Posh"–port cabin out, starboard cabin home–that was the only way to travel in the great days of ocean liners. Cruises to exotic ports departed from cities on the Atlantic and Pacific, and the trip was, for many, the thrill of a lifetime.

In the ship's beauty parlour, fashion-conscious women paid $1.25 for the delicate marcel wave.

Afternoon fashion for the Alaska cruise with the coastal mountains and glacier as backdrop.

Jewel of CP*'s fleet–42,350-ton* Empress of Britain.

Great Escapes

If the problems of the world were too much for you in the thirties, there was at least one great refuge—magazine fiction. In the way that Hollywood had glamourized the relations of its stars, popular monthlies (directed mostly at women) romanticized the great loves of make-believe heroes and heroines. Love with the handsome, exotic and wealthy stranger was the formula to success.

She leaned across the table and asked which one he would like, and he said the fifth from the left.

She leaned across the table and asked which he would like, and he said the fifth from the left.

MIDNIGHT SAILING
By Frederick Nebel

"A stowaway... You know you could be landed at the nearest port and clapped in jail, eh?"

She almost ran across to the desk, and her eyes were that big!

NOT IN OUR Stars

·BY MAUD DIVER·

Impermissible words crowded into his mind, but he only achieved the lame conclusion, "See you tomorrow—the polo match?"

Billie Sue Brister managed a soft laugh. For the first time in years, a man had called her a child. Her! Usually men told her that she was a woman, a reckless, lovely, untamed woman. But Val Haworth was calling her a child.

THE ENCHANTED Chorus Girl BY JOHN CHANCELLOR

Halsey was intensely conscious of the seconds going by, ten minutes that would never come again in the world's history.

Florenz Ziegfeld once told her to "go back to Canada and forget the stage"; the famed D.W. Griffith said she'd never be a movie actress, her eyes were too blue. But Edith Norma Shearer wouldn't listen. The Montreal-born teenager had gone with her mother to New York and played a few bit parts before she caught the eye of movie mogul Irving Thalberg. Throughout the '20s and '30s she was one of Hollywood's greatest sensations.

CHAPTER SIX

Hollywood Believable

If we started giving [Deanna Durbin] dramatic coaching it would probably ruin her.

Hollywood producer

Mass entertainment saved the thirties from being the dark, dreary decade we sometimes imagine. Movies, radio, magazines, and other forms of popular entertainment were more accessible, more brilliant and more seductive than ever. They were out of touch with the real world of soup kitchens and dust storms and relief vouchers, but who wanted to be reminded of reality? They were almost all made in the United States but who cared? If the Americans could give us more laughs, or thrills, or romance for a dime than our own entertainers, more power to them.

In the field of moving pictures, nothing was produced in Canada and there was little of value coming from England. Canadians looked to Hollywood for their movies, and got them by the thousands. Live Canadian shows like The Dumbells, which had toured the country with great success in the twenties, now found theatre rents too high, and Al Plunkett finally had to concede defeat to Bing Crosby, Maurice Chevalier and Lawrence Tibbett. Red Newman and Pat Rafferty had little chance against comedians like the Marx Brothers and W. C. Fields. The only hope for the best Canadian performers was to go south, which they did by the dozens.

Hollywood belonged to Canadians as much as it did to anybody. A dozen or more of the top Hollywood stars were Canadians – Walter Huston, Norma Shearer, Marie Dressler, Mary Pickford, Raymond Massey, Beatrice Lillie, Deanna Durbin, Fay Wray, Fifi D'Orsay and Ned Sparks. There were also many Canadians working as technicians, writers, and extras in the motion picture industry.

Talking pictures had a tremendous impact on Canadian life. They were heavily laden with that special brand of hokum labelled "Hollywood believable." Virtue always triumphed, crime never paid, sin was punished, and true love ended at the altar. Nobody ever bothered to investigate what happened after the marriage, and industry standards would not permit even a married couple to be seen in the same bed together.

The movies affected our language, our manners and our style in subtle ways. When Marlene Dietrich wore long pants on the street, thousands of Canadian women followed suit. When Clark Gable took off his shirt in *It Happened One Night* and revealed he wore no undershirt, the sale of undershirts dropped drastically in stores all over Canada.

For many women sharp profiles, toothy smiles and broad shoulders became the chief criteria of male worth. Mothers wanted their little girls to be frilly and cute and adept at tap dancing. A surprising number of female babies were named

Dancing, romancing Deanna Durbin – born in Winnipeg, she won instant stardom as a teenager in '30s movie musicals like That Certain Age, Mad About Music *and* It's A Date.

Canada in Hollywood

What's more American than Abe Lincoln? Yet Canadian actors Walter Huston and Raymond Massey (above) starred in the role. Nelson Eddy collars the culprit (below) in the 1936 version of *Rose Marie.* The Mountie's girl is Jeanette Macdonald.

Shirley. Canadian men were disappointed by women who did not look like Norma Shearer or Carole Lombard. A sock on the jaw was considered to be the best way of winning an argument, and the police were never wrong. The Hollywood set represented the perfect home, and swimming pools and shiny cars were considered the epitome of the good life.

Jeanette MacDonald in Rose Marie

The "golden age" of the movies witnessed the birth of exceptional films and saw tremendous technical developments, especially in the use of sound. At the beginning of the thirties, sound was squeaky and of limited range; by the end it was just about perfect.

Musicals were a particular delight. Nelson Eddy won the hearts of women from coast to coast when he stood there, so handsome, strong and pure, singing to Jeanette MacDonald in *Rose Marie,* the story of a Canadian Mountie. Eddy and MacDonald were both pretty, and the scenery was breathtaking.

Talkies brought such great plays to the screen as *Journey's End, Anna Christie* and *The Petrified Forest.* Popular novels were also adapted for the medium, including *Arrowsmith, All Quiet on the Western Front, Wuthering Heights, Moby Dick* and *The Wizard of Oz.* There were a number of gangster films which made heroes of bad guys. Although the audiences wept when Jimmy Cagney was gunned down in the last reel, they had a nice safe feeling that justice and the police were watching over them. In 1930 Edward G. Robinson made *Little Caesar* and two years later Paul Muni starred in *Scarface,* based on the career of Al Capone.

In 1931 two horror pictures scared Canadians out of their seats – *Frankenstein* with Boris Karloff and *Dracula* with Bela Lugosi. They began a series of fantastic pictures of which *King Kong* in 1933 was the ultimate. There were several westerns filmed in the thirties, and *Stagecoach* in 1939 set a high standard for others to follow. Carole Lombard and William Powell started a genre of sophisticated comedies in 1936 with *My Man Godfrey,* a zany story about a family of bored millionaires who picked up a butler from the gutter.

Movie audiences of the thirties loved kids. Shirley Temple captivated millions when she sang and danced at the age of five in *Stand Up And Cheer* in 1934. She made an average of four pictures a year, and her salary was $300,000. Her curls were her trademark and six million Shirley Temple dolls were sold at prices from $3 to $30 each.

Another phenomenon of the thirties was the humour of the four Marx Brothers, Groucho, Harpo, Chico, and Zeppo. Their Broadway hit, "The Cocoanuts," took Hollywood by storm. Teenagers had never heard patter so witty, saucy or sardonic, and they broke each other up with Groucho's gags. Playing a hotel desk clerk, Groucho answered the phone and said, "Yes? You want ice water in Room 37? Have you got any ice?" The brothers later dropped Zeppo from the act and went on to make such laugh-producers as *Horsefeathers, Monkey Business, Duck Soup* and the incomparable *A Night at the Opera.*

"Whistle While You Work"

Animated films evolved and prospered. Walt Disney had successes with *Flowers and Trees* and *Three Little Pigs,* and finally produced the fabulous full-length feature, *Snow White.* Canadians and Americans alike sang "Who's Afraid of the Big Bad Wolf" and "Whistle While You Work." And lots of people whistled while they worked.

Nothing like the radio shows of the thirties has ever happened before or since. By 1929, radio brought clear, static-free sound and music into almost every home on the continent. The radio set became the centre of home entertainment, replacing the piano and the phonograph. It was impossible to get a fourth for bridge when Jack Benny was on the air, and to phone a friend on Sunday night, the best radio night of all, was to invite a snarl and a receiver banged down on your ear.

"Hello, folks. This is Jack Benny."

Comedy, drama, sports broadcasts, serials, news and commentary filled the air. The Lone Ranger rode his great white stallion, Silver, into the hearts of millions of children, while sound men sent shivers up and down the listeners' spines with squeaking doors, prying coffin lids, howling hounds, and giant spiders devouring human flesh. Spell-binding preachers like Canadian-born Father Charles E. Coughlin spoke to thirty or forty million at a time and drew 50,000 letters a week.

Everybody had a favourite. For many it was the smooth-haired, nervous comedian who in 1932 walked up to a microphone, took a deep breath and said, "Hello, folks. This is Jack Benny. There will now be a slight pause while everybody says . . . 'Who cares'?" The lack of audience response was almost too much for Benny and he soon realized that he must have live people there in the studio to laugh at his jokes. Thus was the studio audience born, and it became as much a part of the show as the stars themselves.

Benny made accomplished comedians of everybody in his cast. Rochester the butler, girlfriend Mary Livingston, orchestra leader Phil Harris, singer Dennis Day, announcer Don Wilson and soundman Mel Blanc all made Benny the butt of their jokes, ribbing him about his stinginess, his age, his thinning hair, his old Maxwell car, and his romantic pretensions.

The girl in the hairy paw is none other than Fay Wray, known in the business as "a great screamer." When the Alberta-born actress was asked to play the role, she was told she'd be playing opposite the tallest and darkest lead in Hollywood. Naturally she expected it to be Clark Gable.

Stars of the Silver Screen

Glitter! Romance! Stardom! The focus of the entertainment world was Hollywood. Silent movies had become talkies, and the studios were paying a fortune for the girl with the right smile. The lure of "Tinseltown" was irresistible for Canadian talent too; some had already made their reputation, others were willing to take a gamble. Late-show watchers may find a familiar face among these.

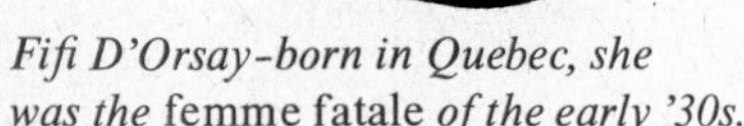

Fifi D'Orsay–born in Quebec, she was the femme fatale *of the early '30s.*

Beatrice Lillie–born in Toronto in 1898, "the mistress of sophisticated slapstick."

Marie Dressler–born in Cobourg, Ont. A star at home, she became Hollywood's "Thunder Chief."

Fay Wray–Alberta-born leading lady of horrors and disasters like "King Kong."

Raymond Massey–one of the world's great actors made his war-time debut in Siberia.

Bobby Breen–child star of '30s musicals, "a singer with the voice of a cherub."

Walter Huston–born in Toronto in 1884, he starred in 30 movies in the '30s.

David Manners–born in Halifax, he wanted to be a sea captain and ended up in films.

Jeanette Loff–she played the piano in a Sask. movie house before she met DeMille.

Fads of the Thirties

Roller skating, contract bridge, Monopoly, miniature golf, dime chain-letters, Hoople cheques and a dozen other crazy notions.

Montreal police took to their bicycles in an effort to curb two-wheeled violators who ignored the rules.

Even the sidewalks were not safe as roller skates became the craze.

Saturday afternoons found kids and adults putting around tiny links like this one in Winnipeg.

Benny could do more with a pause than most comedians could do with a punchline. Accosted by a burglar who demanded "Your money or your life!" he produced the longest pause on radio, during which the laughter built as people caught onto the gag. At just the right second, Benny said, "All right. I'm thinking about it."

Eddie Cantor's wife and daughters were known and loved by millions. When Charlie McCarthy talked to W. C. Fields, the audience could hardly wait for Field's wheezy threat to put Charlie up in the backyard for the woodpeckers.

War of the Worlds

Every Monday night Cecil B. DeMille introduced the *Radio Theatre* from Hollywood on which the best of the movies were adapted for radio, starring cinema greats of the magnitude of Norma Shearer and Ronald Coleman. The best radio drama, however, was that which was written specifically for the medium. The chillers written by Arch Oboler for the show *Lights Out* were the best of their genre ever produced. *Inner Sanctum,* which opened with the squeaking door and the diabolical laugh of Raymond, the host, chilled the blood of millions. Best of all was Orson Welles who produced the incomparable *Mercury Theatre.* On October 30, 1938, Welles presented Howard Koch's adaptation of H. G. Wells' *War of the Worlds* in such a realistic way that millions of people panicked, believing that the Earth was being invaded from outer space.

No actual suffering of the thirties could match that described in the radio serials, twelve minutes of dialogue and three minutes of Hammond organ playing and selling. They began early in the morning and ran all day. In the melodrama of the hungry thirties, dishonest, ruthless, heartless industrialists were the commonest villains. A great favourite was *Big Sister,* which came on at breakfast time and featured a gallant young woman's battle against bad luck, corruption in high places, and wicked big businessmen. The vociferous and meddlesome Ma Perkins was constantly plagued by the problems of her family and friends.

Next only to radio and the movies, the unprecedented number of magazines that flowed from the United States across the border into Canada had a powerful Americanizing effect. Most of the magazines ignored the facts of the Depression and considered their main function to amuse and assure everyone that everything would be all right.

The *Reader's Digest* led the rest. Hardly a Canadian home was without one and scarcely a serious conversation concluded without somebody quoting from it. The January 1930 issue contained ninety-five pages, not a line of advertising and thirty-four articles condensed from other magazines on the last war, raising children, trial marriages, instrument flying, and one obviously written in 1929 entitled "Why We Are Prosperous." By April 1938, the content had not changed significantly. The lead articles were "School for the Brilliant," "Twenty Months in Alcatraz," and "We Formed a Gossip Detective Agency."

a joke magazine called Life

One of the most popular magazines was *Liberty,* a weekly package of fact and fiction which sold for a nickel. Above each article there was a bracketed number indicating how long it would take the average reader to read it. *Liberty* began publishing a Canadian edition in 1932, and its first editorial assistant was required to have shorthand, typing, two years of newspaper experience and a BA degree, all for $12.50 per week.

In 1936 Henry Luce, who was already publishing *Time* and *Fortune,* bought the title and circulation list for a joke magazine called *Life* and filled it with startling photographs of violence, sex, crime and politics. It soon found its weekly way into most Canadian homes, far outselling *Maclean's, Chatelaine, Canadian Home Journal, Saturday Night* and other Canadian magazines.

"the slicks" and "the pulps"

The American women's magazines outsold their Canadian counterparts. *Ladies' Home Journal, McCall's* and *Pictorial Review* advised housewives on child raising, husband care and fashions, but were coy and reticent in discussing sexual relations. The "slicks," a name given to family magazines such as *Saturday Evening Post, Collier's,* and *American Magazine,* ran general articles and light "escape" fiction.

The thirties also witnessed an epidemic of "the pulps", which took their name from the cheap, brownish pulp paper on which they were printed. Edgar Rice Burroughs had written his first Tarzan stories for the pulps. With titles like "Weird Tales," "Ranch Romance," "Fantastic Adventure," and "Love," they were cheap and contained little advertising – mostly about guns or rejuvenating potions.

Tattered copies of pulps with voluptuous nudes or science fiction illustrations on the covers were carried in the packs of the thousands of itinerant workers who roamed the country during the thirties. Depicting better places and better times where a man could accomplish anything if he possessed sufficient resolve, the pulps were often all that sustained a lonely man on the road.

Most of the songs Canadians sang and listened to in the thirties also came wafting across the border. The big bands of Paul Whiteman, Jimmy Dorsey, Benny Goodman and Artie Shaw were well known throughout Canada. They made frequent visits to Montreal, Toronto, Vancouver and Winnipeg and they packed the halls. Banks of clarinetists, trombonists, saxophonists standing in

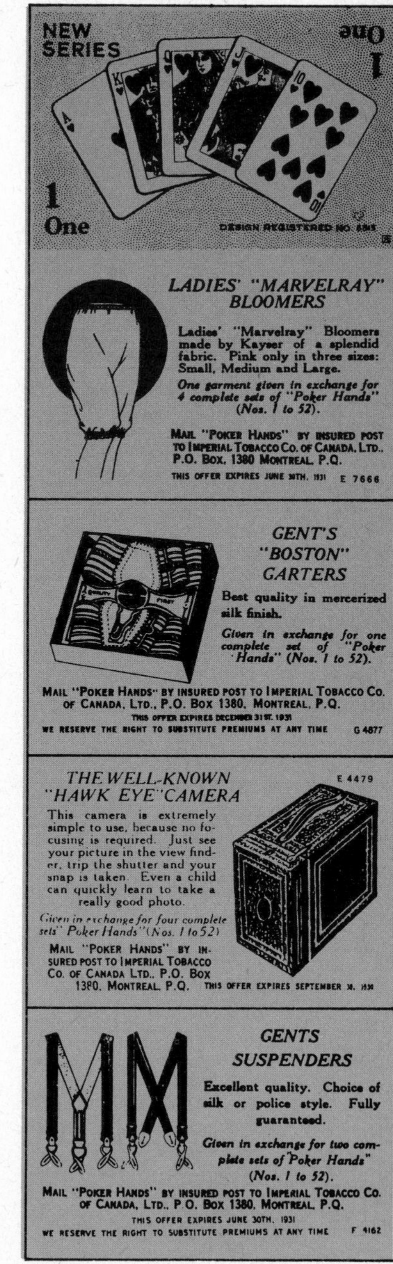

Cigarette-card poker for prizes, courtesy of Imperial Tobacco. Five packs of cigarettes and a bit of luck could get you any one of the practical prizes shown above.

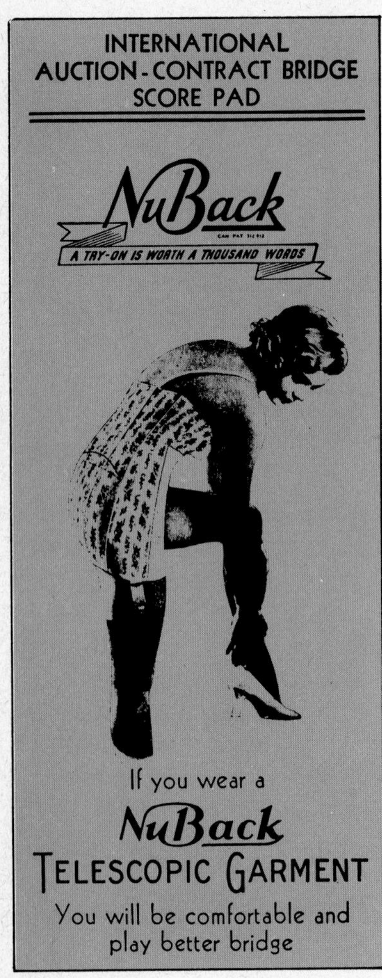

What this "telescopic garment" had to do with playing better bridge only the manufacturer would know.

turn to blast the air with rhythm, and drummers like the incomparable Gene Krupa, would bring the audience to their feet, swaying and screaming and often jumping into the aisles to dance. Then a singer like Frank Sinatra or Connie Boswell would take the spotlight and melt hearts with poignant lyrics. The music was called "swing" and nothing was ever better named.

All over Canada groups of talented but unemployed youths scraped together enough money to form bands. They barnstormed around to the smaller towns, filling the town halls, collecting their twenty-five dollars, loading their instruments into battered old Buicks or Hudsons and moving on to the next one-night stand. Always there was the dream of the big time.

Many of the songs that they sang suggested the hard times of the thirties – "Let's Put Out The Lights," "I Can't Give You Anything But Love," and "I Found a Million Dollar Baby in a Five and Ten Cent Store." Many were romantic such as "You Ought To Be In Pictures," and "Walking in a Winter Wonderland." Others were sheer nonsense like "Goody Goody," "The Music Goes Round and Round" and "Three Little Fishies." While "Begin the Beguine," "Stardust," "Night and Day" and "Stormy Weather" will live for a long, long time.

Every fad or change in manners and fashions that struck the American nation was quickly adopted by Canadians. In the early thirties, when Mr. and Mrs. Ely Culbertson ballyhooed the game of contract bridge into a national mania, Canadians followed suit.

When enterprising promoters turned vacant lots throughout America into miniature golf courses, the same thing happened to Canada. The idea was to get the ball along narrow alleyways, through certain obstacles, and into the holes. The obstacles around the course were decorated with cute figures of Mickey Mouse and Maggie and Jiggs.

The miniature golf craze was short-lived in Canada, and for promoters it was financially disastrous. Regular golf, on the other hand, enjoyed a tremendous boom as working men and the unemployed adopted a game that had previously been played by the rich at private clubs. Many farmers with land near the city found it more profitable to convert their acres into a golf course than to use it raising produce for which there was little market. The greens were often made of oiled sand, and more than one golfer played a round with only a midiron and a putter clutched in his hand. Some cities converted vacant land into municipal golf courses where you could play all day for 50 cents. Because it permitted players to buy and sell, invest, borrow, lend and accumulate without risking a cent of real money, a game called Monopoly became a craze. And for some reason people were going around saying to each other:

"Knock, knock!"
"Who's there?"
"Ivan."
"Ivan who?"
"Ivan Ocean to punch you in the snoot."

Throughout the thirties the little details of daily life in Canada had grown more and more like life in the United States. While the Depression lasted people were so preoccupied with worrying about money or trying to forget it, that little thought was given to this situation.

Opposite page: *Colourful, kinky and packed with adventure, pulp magazines meant entertainment in the hungry thirties. Thousands of these pulps had no trouble getting into Canada from their publishers in the States. But customs and censorship officials sealed the border against anything with "spicy" in the title or a demi-clad body on the cover.*

ARK OF SPACE
THE FORTRESS OF UTOPIA
By JACK WILLIAMSON
DETECTIVE
ALIBI
By J. S. Perry
THREE THRILLING MYSTERY NOVELETTES
ALL THESE MUST DIE!
by W. WAYNE ROBBINS
THE BEAST OF LITTLE BLACK
by HUGH B. CAVE
MARCH OF THE
ST. LOUIS
10¢ DIME MYSTERY
25¢
STORIES for AUGUST
NOVELETTE by RAY CUMMINGS
ZAGAT
DOWST
JAN. 13
10¢
Great New Fantastic Novel by the Author of MINIONS of the MOON
ARGOSY
WEEKLY
Rip-roaring adventure of the Mounties
WHEN the RIVER RAN WHITE
Exciting Fiction by Top-Notch Authors
HARRY SINCLAIR DRAGO
WILLIAM GRAY BEYER
EUSTACE L. ADAMS
SULLIVAN and Many Others
THE Shadow
A STREET & SMITH PUBLICATION
TWICE A MONTH
10¢
DEC. 1st 1938
STORIES
LISTEN TO THE
JAMES - SPERRY
MAGAZINE
RESURRECTION DAY
80-Page Novel
10
SATAN

The Bands We Danced To

The bands we danced to in the thirties were as itinerant as the jobless who "rode the rails." The difference was money, and bands and their leaders had no trouble making ends meet. The bands we danced to were Mart Kenney, Luigi Romanelli, Horace Lapp, Loren Cassina, Ferde Mowry, Guy Lombardo, Fred Culley, Bert Niosi, Trump Davidson, Stan Patton, Jack Slatter, Billy Bissett, and a host of others.

YOU
I SAW STARS
BY
MAURICE SIGLER
AL GOODHART
AL HOFFMAN
Featured by
GUY LOMBARDO
An Old Water Mill
Featured by
Percy Faith
LITTLE WHITE LIES
by WALTER DONALDSON
SOUTH OF THE BORDER
(DOWN MEXICO WAY)
by
JIMMY KENNEDY
and
MICHAEL CARR
PRINTED IN CANADA
Guy Lombardo
ER SMILE AGAIN
RUTH LOWE
Featured by Horace Lapp and his Orchestra at the Royal York Hotel
SOMEBODY ELSE IS TAKING MY PLACE
by
DICK HOWARD,
BOB ELLSWORTH
and
RUSS MORGAN

The HAPPY GANG

GEORGE TEMPLE BLAIN MATHE BOB FARNON
EDDIE ALLEN BERT PEARL KAY STOKES HUGH BARTLETT

CHAPTER SEVEN

The Magic of Radio

To us the CBC was *Canada, all the things during the Depression that weren't bleak and all around us.*

Al Johnson, president of the CBC, 1976

In the early evening of April 20, 1936, while some Canadians finished dinner and others were still at work, radio listeners heard a deep voice saying:

This is the Canadian Radio Commission calling Canada from Moose River. Herman Magill is dead. Others still in the depths of the mine . . . can hear the men in the workings breaking down the rocks to get through to them.

It was the voice of J. Frank Willis in the first of his regular five minute bulletins from the pit head at Moose River, Nova Scotia. Some people sat by their radios day and night until the dramatic climax of the story three days later., Canadian radio came of age. The Canadian Radio Broadcasting Commission had been appointed by the Bennett government in 1933 to counteract the influence of pervasive American radio programming. The Commission had done a creditable job of bringing recitals and concerts to the public, along with broadcasts by Canadian and British government leaders, including King George V, but it had not as yet lured many listeners away from American programmes.

The Moose River Mine Disaster was the big chance to get the ear of most Canadians and millions in the United States as well, and the Commission made the most of it. Every Canadian with a radio set was there through the voice of J. Frank Willis.

On the evening of April 12, 1936, two Toronto men, Dr. David E. Robertson, chief surgeon at the Hospital for Sick Children, and Herman R. Magill, thirty-year-old lawyer and broker, went to inspect a mine they had bought in Moose River, a tiny settlement deep in the bush and rock country, sixty miles northeast of Halifax.

With their timekeeper, Alfred Scadding, also from Toronto, the men descended the mine to the 370-foot level. Here they were alarmed by the noise of shifting rock and decided to get out as quickly as possible. They took the skip to the 140-foot level, but found the roof caved in. Thev were trapped in a dark, wet, underground cave. Rescue operations seemed hopeless until the third day when, with great persistence, a diamond drill operator named Billy Bell managed to get a small hole down to the men and a telephone line was lowered. The trapped men reported that Magill had died from exposure; the other two were alive but suffering from cold, wet and hunger.

When newspaper coverage became extensive, a representative of the Columbia Broadcasting System had phoned Dupont J. Arthur of the Canadian

Premier Protests False Radio News

The following telegram was despatched yesterday:
HALIFAX, NOVA SCOTIA, APRIL 21 1936
CANADIAN RADIO COMMISSION
OTTAWA
SPEAKING I BELIEVE FOR MANY PEOPLE WHO HAVE EXPRESSED ANNOYANCE AT METHODS FOLLOWED BY SOME RADIO ANNOUNCERS IN COMMENTING ON MOOSE RIVER MINE CALAMITY I PROTEST AGAINST INACCURATE EXAGGERATED AND OVER DRAMATIZED NATURE OF SOME RADIO COMMENTS STOP PEOPLE OF PROVINCE ARE NATURALLY WARM HEARTED AND SYMPATHETIC AND IN COMMON WITH MILLIONS OF OTHERS IN WORLD ARE DEEPLY STIRRED BY PLIGHT ENTOMBED MEN STOP THEY HAVE RIGHT TO RECEIVE ALL INFORMATION BUT I THINK THEY ALSO HAVE A RIGHT TO ACCURATE INFORMATION AND NOT SUPPOSITIONS BROADCAST BY MEN OF NO EXPERIENCE WHATEVER IN MINING MATTERS STOP NEITHER SHOULD FALSE HOPES BE RAISED NOR GROUNDLESS FEARS ENGENDERED IN ALREADY ANGUISHED HEARTS IN THE ATTEMPT TO BE DRAMATIC AND SENSATIONAL.
ANGUS L. MACDONALD
PREMIER OF NOVA SCOTIA

Frank Willis' reporting of the Moose River disaster was hailed by some as an historic moment in radio. Others felt that "yellow journalism" had reached the juvenile CRBC.

Opposite page: *"Knock, knock." "Who's there?" "It's the Happy Gang!" CBC's musical merrymakers from 1937 to 1957–two decades of radio fun.*

Disaster at Moose River

The tiny gold-mining town of Moose River, Nova Scotia, became the focus of world interest for 58 hours and 2 minutes on April 20, 1936, while rescuers struggled to save the three trapped men.

CRBC's "you are there" reporter, Frank Willis, on mike with draegerman Billy Bedaux at the mine shaft.

Three men struggle to stay alive as the water rises, 141 feet below the surface of the earth.

Radio Broadcasting Commission, requesting a radio "feed" from Moose River, and saying that if he could not get one he would make his own arrangements. Arthur saw the opportunity for a scoop and decided to send a crew to do the job. It consisted of his Maritimes programme director, J. Frank Willis, Arleigh Canning, a CRBC engineer, and Cecil Landry, an announcer-engineer from CHNS, Halifax. They were driven to the site over slippery, rutted, dirt roads by Louis Murphy in his Graham Page Straight Eight motor car, equipped with one of the first sets of winter tread tires ever used. They arrived at the mine on Monday, April 20.

fifty million of them listened

Immediately Willis found that he would have to fight for his rights. Not only had the Toronto papers sent squads of reporters, but there were men there from the news services and just about every good-sized city in North America. To add to his difficulties there was only one telephone line – a party line at that – connecting the mine with Halifax and hence with the rest of the world.

Fortunately, the top-ranking official at the site, Michael Dwyer, Minister of Mines for Nova Scotia, arbitrarily commandeered the telephone line, cut off the thirteen party-line subscribers and worked out a schedule whereby Willis could have it for five minutes every half hour for a broadcast.

Willis had a tremendous advantage over his competitors. His bosses hooked up a fifty-eight-station Canadian network and sold the service to the three leading American networks comprising some 650 stations. This meant that almost anyone on the North American continent who could get to a radio could hear what was going on at the exact moment it happened.

An estimated fifty million of them listened. A lawyer in St. Andrews, Quebec, later wrote that he had not slept at all through three nights of the broadcast. At Fort William the officers and men of the Canadian Legion listened in a group; all three trapped men were or had been soldiers. Teachers set up radios in their classrooms. Housewives phoned their husbands at work to give them the news. Miners, fishermen, farmers and Arctic adventurers listened, worried and prayed for the safety of the men.

the Calvary of anguish

Everybody knew the men were alive. People at the site could talk to them and send them food, but they could not get them out. Because of the unstable nature of the rock and the constant water seepage, there was always danger of another cave-in. Hard rock miners came to help from Stellarton, a hundred miles north, and from northern Ontario. The rescuers were using dynamite, and dynamite is always dramatic. Every weary miner or harassed official emerging from the diggings was pounced upon by reporters and his story sent out to the waiting millions. Some said the men would be up in minutes, others said hours, others couldn't tell. Willis said:

I won't try to paint a mental picture of what is going on underground . . . the torture of doubt, the Calvary of mental and physical anguish, the nerve-destroying sound of dripping water, the rattle and splash of falling rock chips.

Standing there in his black overcoat with the upturned collar and his grey fedora, less than fifteen feet from the mouth of the hole, Willis grabbed the draegermen as they crawled out and brought them to his hand-held circular mike. Dr. H.K. McDonald of Halifax, who was in charge of feeding the trapped men, described how they had been given "chocolate, coffee, corn syrup, vitone." He also said he expected the men to be up within a few minutes. Now and then Willis would pause so that the listeners could hear the actual pulsating of the pump that was sending life-giving air down to the entombed men.

Finally came this bulletin from a breathless Willis:

Ladies and Gentlemen, this is the Canadian Radio Commission calling North America from Moose River. I have just run from the pit head. There is no longer any element of doubt. The rescue has been accomplished. This long-looked-for victory is now in our hands, and those men are coming out alive!

After 58 hours and 2 minutes of broadcast time, Willis signed off, so tired that he could hardly speak. He had done it all alone – no writer, no prepared script, practically no relief. He had eaten when he could and slept in cold, drafty bunks when he could grab a minute. He did his own leg work, fought with newspapermen and put up with inexperienced interviewees. He had drawn fifty million people into this drama of human survival. When he came to talk about Magill, the man who had died, his voice failed completely. "It's almost more than I can bear to say. We're cutting our wires now and heading back."

the Aird Commission

It was just six months after Willis' magnificent Moose River broadcasts that the Canadian Broadcasting Corporation was born.

The first steps had been taken back in 1928 when the Mackenzie King government appointed a Royal Commission, under the chairmanship of Sir John Aird, president of the Canadian Bank of Commerce, to examine the broadcasting situation. The Aird Commission studied broadcasting in the United States, Britain, Germany, France, Belgium, and the Irish Free State. They held public sessions in twenty-five Canadian cities, heard 164 verbal

Gordon Sinclair
A Man Who Wouldn't Sit Down

When the depression was at its worst in Canada, a thirty-three-year-old wandering Toronto *Star* reporter, Gordon Sinclair, was "loose among devils, in quest of cannibals, and footloose in India." Born in 1900 in Toronto's "Cabbagetown" – "North America's biggest anglo-saxon slum" – he was a high school dropout. During his tempestuous teens he worked in a dozen different places, from the Bank of Nova Scotia to a slaughterhouse. In his early twenties he wangled his way into the post of Women's Editor at the *Star,* admitted he knew nothing about women, and four years later found himself on the road, doing a series of first-hand stories about hoboes. The *Star*'s readers loved them. The editors, picking up on a good thing, sent him to Europe, then to the Orient, and around the world four times, receiving lively articles in return. As a reporter during WW II, he was not popular with the military establishment, but in August 1942 Toronto's CFRB asked him to do a radio series on the war, "Headlines." It was the start of a meteoric rise.

Foster Hewitt
The Voice of Hockey

Radio was relatively new in March '23 when nineteen-year-old Foster Hewitt gave his first play-by-play account of the action from Toronto's Mutual Street Arena. It was the third time anyone had tried such a thing (Norm Albert and Pete Parker were the first only a month before). But the young *Star* reporter took to the CFCA mike without flinching. He already had some radio experience with Ottawa's CFGO, and sports, of course, was the main topic in the Hewitt household. His father, Bill, had been at the *Star*'s sports desk for years, and he himself was a champ in his own right, undefeated as a boxer on the inter-collegiate circuit. By the early '30s Foster Hewitt was already known as the voice of hockey. He had covered other events too: the British air-ship *R-100* at St. Hubert and the maiden voyage of the *Empress of Britain*. But when the Maple Leaf Gardens was finished in '31, the broadcast booth was a permanent feature and Foster became a fixture within the fixture.

statements and received 124 written briefs. Their report, submitted in September of 1929, had recommended the establishment of a national system.

In order that this report would not be shelved, as so many Royal Commission reports had been, a group of citizens led by Graham Spry and Alan B. Plaunt formed a Canadian Radio League to work for a nationalized radio system. Their hope was that radio in Canada would not be controlled by advertisers, as it was in the United States, and that it would become a potent weapon against the American cultural invasion.

There was a sort of semi-public radio network in Canada encompassing a number of private stations and operated by the Canadian National Railway. On January 21, 1930, this network broadcast the opening of the Naval Conference in London, England, featuring a speech by King George V. It was the first time the King's voice was heard across Canada. The network sponsored health talks by the Canadian Medical Association and an All-Canada Symphony Hour. It covered the unveiling of the monument to General Wolfe in Quebec City, the arrival of the British dirigible, *R-100*, and the arrival of the new Governor General, the Earl of Bessborough, in April 1931.

erudite editor of Saturday Night

Prime Minister Bennett was greatly concerned over the "insidious American influence" of radio. The Canadian Broadcasting Act, which became law on May 26, 1932, was described by one veteran broadcaster as the most significant accomplishment of Bennett's five years in office. In September of that year, a message had gone out from the Prime Minister's office to Hector Willoughby Charlesworth, the jaunty, erudite editor of *Saturday Night* magazine, offering Charlesworth the position of Chairman of the Canadian Radio Broadcasting Commission with a blank paper on which to work out his own ideas in his own way. In this way the principle of freedom from government interference in the public broadcasting system had been firmly established.

Charlesworth accepted the position and the first major CRBC broadcast was at Christmas in 1932 when Canadians from coast to coast heard their King send each of them a message of good cheer and best wishes, complete with the chiming of Big Ben and the sound of London traffic in the background. Radio reached into many rural homes where no newspapers or magazines ever came. Radio was immediate. Taping of shows was a long way off and everything was "live." If a speaker or announcer made a slip of the tongue, it had to stand, as when one called the British statesman Sir Stafford Cripps, "Sir Stifford Crapps," and another referred to the A and P Food Stores as "The A and Poo Feed Stores."

Max Baer and Jim Braddock

Canadians heard the voices of George Bernard Shaw, Rudyard Kipling, the Prince of Wales, Lord Baden-Powell and Allan Roy Dafoe. They heard Haile Selassie of Ethiopia appealing to the world for support against Mussolini's "daring" airmen who were bombing his villages. They were present at the funeral of the most popular comedian of the day, Will Rogers, and the world heavyweight championship fight between Max Baer and Jim Braddock. They heard with tremendous sorrow of the death of King George V and were present at his funeral. Radio united the nation in a way that newspapers and magazines never could. The climax of the story was the Mackenzie King government's 1936 Broadcasting Act which gave birth to the Canadian Broadcasting Corporation. Now there was more money available to increase the extent and quality of the coverage, and new powerful stations were built at strategic points across the country to give better reception.

Saturday night brought "Hockey Night in Canada," with Foster Hewitt describing the play-by-play action. Hewitt's enthusiastic style made him universally popular, and when he described a rush by defenceman Red Horner or a save by George Hainsworth, Canadians coast to coast felt that they were actually in the rink.

The announcers oozed dignity and authority. Each evening the sonorous voice of Charles Jennings announced the news from Spain, Berlin, Rome, New York and Ottawa. Jennings would then forecast the weather, beginning at Belle Isle and not stopping until he got to Victoria.

"It's the Happy Gang!"

After lunch one day in June of 1937, came the sound of somebody knocking briskly on a door. A cheerful voice shouted, "Who's there?" and the answer came back, "It's the Happy Gang!" *The Happy Gang* was heard Monday through Friday for many, many years to come. The show was fast and breezy and full of corn. MC Bert Pearl carried the banter and sang a few songs, most of which he had composed himself. Kay Stokes – everybody's Aunt Doris – played the organ, and Eddie Allan sang nice boyish songs and said "Hello, Gram." Bob Farnon played trumpet and joined in the singing, while Blain Mathe played the violin and didn't say much. Hugh Bartlett, the announcer, sold soap and told jokes on the side. He got them out of "the joke pot," which was constantly refilled by people sending in their own favourite corn. The joke pot and the many requests that were sung conveyed the feeling that the show belonged to the people, and at its peak the people sent in some thousand letters a week.

The CBC ventured into comedy with a show called *Woodhouse and Hawkins,* for which Art

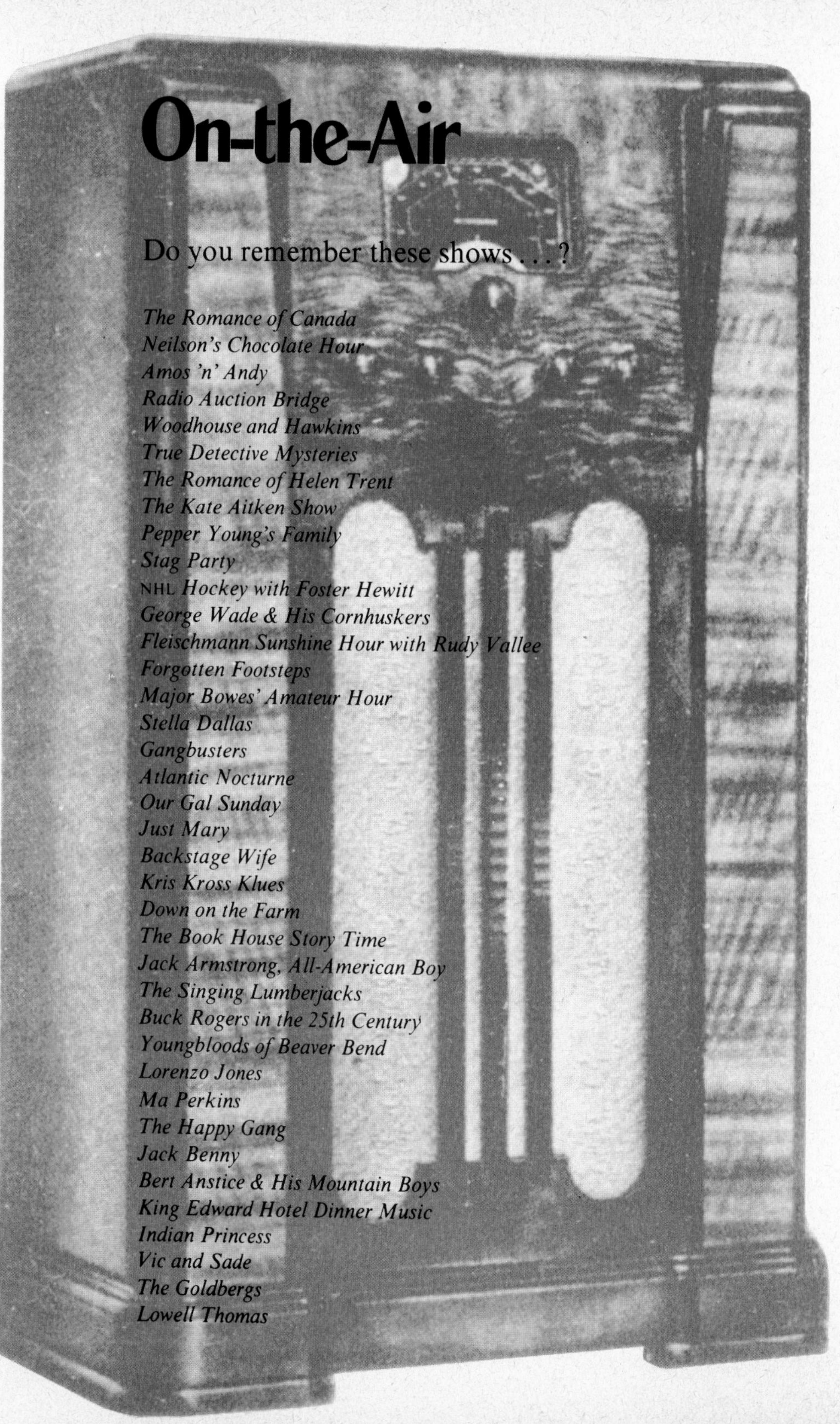

On-the-Air

Do you remember these shows . . . ?

The Romance of Canada
Neilson's Chocolate Hour
Amos 'n' Andy
Radio Auction Bridge
Woodhouse and Hawkins
True Detective Mysteries
The Romance of Helen Trent
The Kate Aitken Show
Pepper Young's Family
Stag Party
NHL *Hockey with Foster Hewitt*
George Wade & His Cornhuskers
Fleischmann Sunshine Hour with Rudy Vallee
Forgotten Footsteps
Major Bowes' Amateur Hour
Stella Dallas
Gangbusters
Atlantic Nocturne
Our Gal Sunday
Just Mary
Backstage Wife
Kris Kross Klues
Down on the Farm
The Book House Story Time
Jack Armstrong, All-American Boy
The Singing Lumberjacks
Buck Rogers in the 25th Century
Youngbloods of Beaver Bend
Lorenzo Jones
Ma Perkins
The Happy Gang
Jack Benny
Bert Anstice & His Mountain Boys
King Edward Hotel Dinner Music
Indian Princess
Vic and Sade
The Goldbergs
Lowell Thomas

Radio: Behind the Scenes

Radio – a decade after the old crackly crystal set. New Westinghouse Pilots and Stromberg-Carlsons stood in the corners of living rooms across Canada. In the evenings the family would gather around and listen. The human voice was actually being transmitted into their homes with remarkable fidelity! But the work that went on in radio studios was even more remarkable. Sound effects men, actors, technicians and announcers all huddled around waiting for their cues.

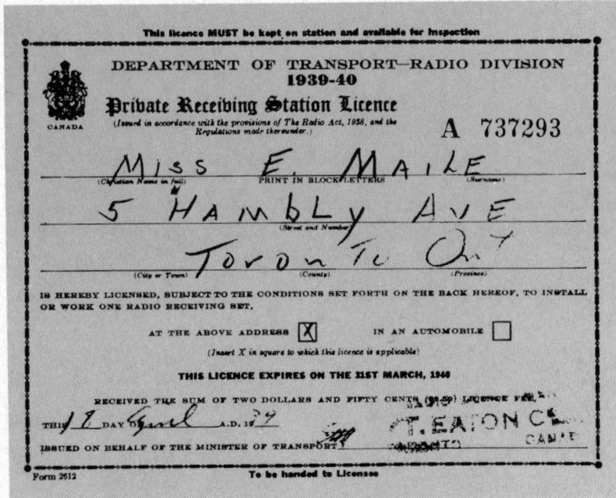

This licence MUST be kept on station and available for inspection

CANADA

DEPARTMENT OF TRANSPORT—RADIO DIVISION
1939-40

Private Receiving Station Licence

(Issued in accordance with the provisions of The Radio Act, 1938, and the Regulations made thereunder.)

A 737293

MISS E. MAILE
(Christian Name in full) PRINT IN BLOCK LETTERS (Surname)

5 HAMBLY AVE
(Street and Number)

Toronto Ont
(City or Town) (County) (Province)

IS HEREBY LICENSED, SUBJECT TO THE CONDITIONS SET FORTH ON THE BACK HEREOF, TO INSTALL OR WORK ONE RADIO RECEIVING SET,

AT THE ABOVE ADDRESS [X] IN AN AUTOMOBILE [ ]

(Insert X in square to which this licence is applicable)

THIS LICENCE EXPIRES ON THE 31ST MARCH, 1940

RECEIVED THE SUM OF TWO DOLLARS AND FIFTY CENTS ($2.50) LICENCE FEE,

THIS 12 DAY OF April A.D. 1939

ISSUED ON BEHALF OF THE MINISTER OF TRANSPORT

T. EATON CO.

Form 2612

To be handed to Licensee

Following British example, government in the '30s tried to pay CBC costs through $2.50 licence fees.

CBC's sound effects crew from '38 (left to right): Bert Stanley, Fred Tudor, Gord Tanner, Harold Symes.

The cast of the 1932 CNR production of "Henry Hudson" shouted out their lines in the first major drama series for the network.

Hudson's Bay Company officials present the new monarchs with beaver pelts as token rent. The '39 tour was covered coast-to-coast by radio.

Vancouver's "Stag Party" brought to radio a star-studded cast. Among the talent featured was Alan Young (left).

Far from the crowds and reporters, the Duke and Duchess of Windsor stroll outside their Alberta ranch. For the woman he loved, Edward VIII gave up the crown, the fanfare and a touch of class when he announced his intention to wed divorcee Wallis Simpson. It was the love story of the decade, if not of the century.

MacGregor and Frank Daville wrote the script and narrated up to twenty different voices, including Lord Percy, the sillyass Englishman, Major Oftenbroke, the pompous fraud, and Egbert, the Major's valet. MacGregor and Daville produced their own sound effects and were funny enough to hold their own against the comedy coming from the American networks.

"Just Mary" stories

Talented young people found in radio an exciting new show business medium and they made the most of it. They organized variety shows, often, it must be admitted, in the image of Jack Benny or Fred Allen, persuaded the local radio station to put them on the air, at no pay of course, and were ready for the CBC representative when auditions were held across the country. It was from these auditions that *Stag Party* starring Alan Young was born in Vancouver. In the Maritimes, a school teacher by the name of Mary Grannan began telling stories every Sunday morning over the radio, and "Just Mary" stories were soon the favourites with children from coast to coast.

There is little doubt that the radio broadcast that most deeply affected listeners during the thirties was the one that began, "At long last I am able to say a few words of my own." It was the voice of a man who wanted to marry an American divorced woman and who, because of that wish, had to abdicate the British throne. On the eleventh day of December, 1936, Edward VIII, soon to become simply the Duke of Windsor, continued:

I have never wanted to withold anything, but until now it has not been constitutionally possible for me to speak. And you must believe me when I tell you that I have found it impossible to carry on the heavy duties and responsibilities and to discharge my duties as King as I would wish to do without the help and support of the woman I love. And now we all have a new king. I wish him and you, his people, happiness and prosperity with all my heart. God bless you all. God save the King!

Three years later, the CBC faced the demanding task of covering the Royal Tour to Canada by the new King, George VI, and Queen Elizabeth.

It was the first visit of a reigning monarch to Canada, and the people wanted to hear it all. From the time George and Elizabeth stepped ashore at Halifax on May 17 until they left six weeks later, their every move was described in hushed and reverent tones. There were 91 broadcasts in all. Radio listeners heard the royal couple being greeted by the mayor of Halifax, heard them in the House of Commons in Ottawa, heard a choir singing "Land of Hope and Glory" at the station in Saskatoon, went with them to visit an Indian teepee in Calgary and listened with fond smiles as the Queen said on the day of departure, "I cannot leave Canada without saying a word of farewell to you all, and thanking you for your wealth of affection offered us through these unforgettable weeks."

Although by the end of the decade, the annual licence fee that was supposed to pay for the broadcasts was dropped in favour of regular parliamentary grants, and the CBC began selling advertising to help defray expenses, the network had done the job for which it had been established. It provided service for remote areas that otherwise would have had none; it organized "forums" for farmers, labour, consumers, and other groups, and made it possible for politicians to speak directly to voters all over Canada. It ended isolation. By 1940 almost 90 per cent of Canadians were reached by CBC broadcasts. Most important of all, the CBC was a powerful force in establishing a sense of unity throughout Canada and counteracting the American influence.

The specially built silver and blue royal train, streamlined and elegant.

Anything showing the royal couple seemed appropriate for the occasion, even a souvenir button of the '37 Coronation.

Royal Tour '39

No expense was too great, no detail too small when in May 1939 George VI and The Queen stepped ashore in Quebec. It was the first Canadian tour of a reigning monarch, and the country went all out. After it was all over, the memories and the memorabilia still remained.

The Bank of Toronto celebrated the event with an item useful in the pre-ballpoint-pen days of the thirties–a blotter.

Fashion Fling

What the well-dressed woman wore in the '30s came from the fashion capitals of the world–Paris, Rome and London. The flat silhouette of the twenties was out! The waist returned to mid-figure with the new fitted fashions, but the hemline dropped back to mid-calf. Corsets and undergarments accentuated the natural curves (and added lines where none had been apparent for a full decade). Yards of material went into the full-skirted look, while the bodice remained tailored throughout the period. In '33 designers exaggerated the broad, square-shoulder look with high neckline and fitted sleeves. Suits followed the fashion in men's clothes, but jackets were closer-fitting and shorter in length. Slacks were worn only around the home or for sports. Hats varied with the whims of milliners, from the Basque beret to the flamboyant pompadour hat of the Duchess of Windsor. By mid-decade veils, nets and cauls were *de rigueur,* and flowers, bows and plumes added an accent of flair. High spiked heels were the mode in footwear, and fashionable women all wore gloves. Cosmetics, especially nail polish, added a bold finishing touch.

Hemlines dropped in the early '30s to six-to-eight inches off the ground (right). The "covered-up look" was back, still borrowing from the straight lines of the '20s but in '33 already showing the square-shoulder style that dominated the decade. By 1939 (above) necklines became more daring, especially in evening wear, and yards of crepe, velvet and sheer organza went into flowing gowns.

Travel costumes for spring 1939 show the hemline once again on the rise. Brighter colours began to reappear in cottons and tweeds, and pink became the fashion rage. Note the knee-length skirts, coats and the fitted, tailored jacket.

By the end of the decade, women's styles had changed radically. Compare the frocks at the bottom of the opposite page with those above. Note also the changes in hair style and the narrow waists.

Around 1938, the shirtwaist dress came into vogue, introducing a new, young and näive look into business and afternoon fashion.

CHAPTER EIGHT

The Floating Island of Newfoundland

The first time I saw a fisherman literally staggering from hunger, my ordinary political instincts collapsed.

Joey Smallwood on 1932 election campaign

Few regions of North America suffered more cruelly in the thirties than did the self-governing Dominion of Newfoundland. And in few places was the reaction more drastic and violent. On April 5, 1932 the streets of St. John's were jammed by a shouting, cursing mob that marched on the House of Parliament and almost wrecked the stately old building with its graceful columns of Irish limestone. The mob fought with the police and tried to lynch the prime minister, or at the very least drown him in the harbour. Eye witnesses who remember the riot are still convinced that if the mob had gotten hold of Sir Richard Squires that evening, they would have killed him, and it was only through the heroic efforts of a small band of clergymen that they were prevented from so doing.

The immediate cause of the riot was the scandal that had hit Squires' government. Charges had been made by Squires' own Minister of Finance, Peter Cashin, that the prime minister had diverted $10,000 of government funds to finance his own political campaigns. The immediate result of the riot was the collapse of responsible government in Newfoundland.

Shortly after the riot, when it was evident that he could no longer lead the government, Squires resigned and in the ensuing general election, the opposition captured a landslide victory with the promise that the island would be placed under a form of commission government appointed from Britain. For the next fifteen years Newfoundlanders would have no say in their government and the island would be under a dictatorship.

But the riots were just the surface cause and consequence of Newfoundland's malaise. The Squire scandal focussed the anger of a destitute and desperate populace whose leaders had brought the island to the point of collapse. The people were starving, the Treasury was bankrupt and none of the politicians – not Squires, not Cashin, not the leader of the opposition – knew where to go from there.

The Depression hit Newfoundland with the fury of a howling nor-easter. It destroyed the fish market upon which the outport Newfoundlanders depended, greatly curtailed the iron mining operations on Bell Island and ruined the market for pulp and paper.

The outport people were the hardest hit. The outport villages that had grown up over the centuries on the innumerable inlets and coves along Newfoundland's rocky coast usually consisted of a dozen or more sturdy, square, pastel-coloured houses with flat roofs and no basements,

Atlantic Canada and Newfoundland did not escape hard times. With their industries cut and with lean markets for fish, Maritimers had to tighten their belts to survive.

Opposite page: *Port Union docks, Newfoundland. The Island, not yet part of Canada, floating between Great Britain and the Dominion, almost sank in the thirties under the weight of the Depression.*

Cod-Liver Oil

I'm a young married man
and I'm tired of life,
Ten years I've been wed to
a pale sickly wife,
She has nothing to do only
sit down and cry,
Praying, oh praying to God
she would die.

A friend of my own came to
see me one day,
He told me my wife she was
pining away;
He afterwards told me that she
would get strong,
If I'd get a bottle from
dear Doctor John.

I bought her a bottle just
for to try,
The way that she drank it I
thought she would die,
I bought her another, it
vanished the same,
And then she took cod-liver oil
on the brain.

I bought her another she drank
it no doubt,
And then she began to get
terrible stout,
And when she got stout of course
she got strong,
And then I got jealous of
dear Doctor John.

Oh Doctor, oh Doctor, oh dear
Doctor John,
Your cod-liver oil is so pure
and so strong,
I'm afraid of my life I'll go down
in the soil,
If my wife don't stop drinking
your cod-liver oil.

Our house it resembled a big
doctor's shop,
It was covered with bottles from
bottom to top,
And early in the morning when
the kettle do boil,
You'll swear it was singin' of
cod-liver oil.

Somehow this 19th-century Irish ditty has become embedded in the culture of Newfoundland.

perched precariously on the rocks, facing every-which way and joined together by narrow, rocky, often steep paths. There was always a church, sometimes a school, and usually a general store.

The outport fishermen operated almost entirely on a system of credit. At the beginning of each fishing season they went to the merchants and acquired their nets, gasoline, repairs, and enough flour and sugar and other staples to keep them. In return they sold their entire catch to the merchants and, theoretically, collected any balance in their favour. Rarely, of course, was there ever any balance.

As the Depression continued, many outporters with no savings or reserves of any kind found themselves in desperate straits. The price of fish dropped to $1.40 for a quintel of 112 pounds, and even at less than one cent per pound there was little market for it.

heavy, dark "dole bread"

The relief, or dole as it was called, amounted to 6 cents per person per day. This was given not as cash but as vouchers at the local store. What could be bought with the vouchers was carefully prescribed – flour, beans, peas, molasses and fat back pork. The flour was a special whole wheat, fortified product, and housewives detested the heavy, dark "dole bread" that it produced.

There were no such things as fresh vegetables or fresh fruits during the winter months and many people suffered from rickets, beriberi, scurvy and tuberculosis. As Joey Smallwood said, "You'd have to invent another word other than 'depression' to describe what our people went through." Some of the death certificates of the period actually stated "starvation" as the cause of death.

It was not all gloom, of course. The outporters had always been great visitors. Not formal visits in any way, but just casual dropping in to sit on the bench beside the kitchen stove and maybe talk and maybe not. "Times is hard" they would say, and pass on some gossip about how the teacher wasn't getting any pay at all or how the preacher had run out of gas up the coast and could not make the Sunday service. A housewife would offer a slice of dole bread soaked in grease with the apology, "It's all we have dese times, my dear."

Entertainment and recreation were home grown. When neighbours gathered for a "time," self-taught fiddlers and accordionists would produce their instruments and everybody from toddlers to grandparents would join in the dance. There might even be a bit of rum, for smuggling from the nearby French colonies of St. Pierre and Miquelon greatly increased during the thirties.

As the Depression wore on, times got harder. Boats became more dilapidated, nets wore out and there was no gasoline to drive the "make and break" engines. Now and then a fisherman would row out to the fishing grounds in his dory, jig for cod or set out a few traps, but mostly they stayed ashore, often sitting in their unpainted fish shacks telling yarns about the old days and wondering what was happening to their world.

worse than in the outports

In the larger towns and cities conditions were in some ways worse than in the outports. At least the outporter owned his own house and sometimes had a small plot of ground where he could grow potatoes and raise chickens or ducks or geese. The unemployed workers from the pulp mills of Cornerbrook and Grand Falls or the factories and commercial establishments of St. John's depended entirely on the pitifully small dole to support their families.

Because of the destruction of trade, traffic through the port of St. John's was reduced to a trickle, and unemployment was as high as 40 per cent. According to police diaries, much of the greatly increased crime involved the theft of food and clothing.

Some of those who were lucky enough to have work sympathized with the unemployed, while others feared and detested them. When John P. Horwood, who was working for a coal company and was reasonably well off, met a friend on the street and saw that he had no shoes on his feet, he gave the friend $10 to buy a pair. When the unemployed man took the cash to the shoe store, not only was he closely questioned as to where he had got it but the storekeeper reported the case to the relief officer and the unfortunate man was cut off the dole.

Two other unemployed friends exchanged work, one repairing a fence and the other doing some carpentry. When the relief officer discovered they were both "working" he cut them off the dole.

tremendous debt existed

The effect of the Depression on Newfoundland politics was even more drastic than it was on the people. There was no income tax and very little land tax. The bulk of the money raised by the government came from a tariff that was levied on every article imported into the country. Since there were no municipal councils in the outports, all the money for bridges, roads, schools and public necessities came from the central government in St. John's. The local elected member, often not a resident of his constituency and coming there only at election time, was the direct source of these funds. Under such a system it was inevitable that there would be a certain amount of political patronage.

The central government was never able to raise enough money to satisfy the needs of the country. A tremendous debt existed still from the railroad that had been built at the turn of the century and

A way of life for centuries, fishing and whaling became more important than usual during hard times. Here a group of outport whalers work over the week's or month's catch for food and fuel.

The only way to go. Before passable roads connected villages with towns and cities, you just had to do your best when you had places to go. Here's a novel idea for crossing Placentia Gut.

from Newfoundland's magnificent World War I effort. Newfoundland's credit had been good, however, and as deficits occurred the government simply borrowed money to cover them. By 1930 the national debt amounted to $100 million. The semi-annual interest payments alone were more than $3 million.

Blow the Man Down

April 5, 1932. Ten thousand unemployed irate citizens, fired up by allegations that Prime Minister Squires had diverted public money, marched on the old Colonial Building. The PM escaped with his life but his political career was dead.

diverted $10,000 of government funds

When the government of Sir Richard Squires went to the banks for their usual loan in 1931, the loan was flatly refused. The well had run dry. Yet the interest payments had to be made, and the dole was costing a further $1.5 million a year. The country was literally bankrupt.

One obvious solution was to default on the debt. As a self-governing member of the British Commonwealth of Nations, however, Newfoundland could not do that. Britain was under no obligation to come to the island's aid, and countries that do not pay their debts, just like individuals, cannot easily borrow money again.

It was at this point that Peter Cashin made his explosive charge that Squires had diverted $10,000 of government funds to his own use. Cashin was a thunderous speaker, relentless in debate. Like most politicians who in those pre-television days depended on voice and presence to move a crowd, he was a devastating speaker. In his charges, he referred to his colleagues as "men brazen, persistent, wily, crooked and criminal."

The news spread quickly along the streets of St. John's. The unemployed were upset by the charges of corruption. The press and prominent citizens were greatly troubled, and the Protestant and Catholic clergy were outraged.

On April 5, 1932, following an inflammatory protest meeting in the Majestic Theatre downtown, an angry mob of 10,000 unemployed led by a group of prominent citizens marched to the beautiful old Colonial Building on Military Road to present a list of grievances to the Assembly.

A delegation of four entered the Colonial Building to present their petition at the bar of the Chamber. Meanwhile, however, the mob was becoming restless, and some tried to force their way into the building. The police charged with swinging batons, further infuriating the crowd, and soon stones and bricks and pieces of picket fence were flying through the air. Police swung their batons with abandon at any head that happened to be close.

"Where's Squires?"

After a while some of the members, Peter Cashin among them, came out and were given loud cheers. Then somebody shouted "Where's Squires?" and the chant was taken up by the mob. "Take the bastard down to the harbour and drown him."

In the meantime some of the crowd managed to get into the building through a side door and loot the offices. Grand pianos, chairs and desks were thrown out through the windows and smashed. Books and records were piled up and set alight but luckily, somebody managed to put out the fire.

Squires and some of his closest supporters had fled into the big, square speaker's room and barred the door. With Squires was Joey Smallwood, Lady Squires and the chief of police. Rocks and bricks were hitting the drawn curtains of the speaker's room and it would only be a matter of minutes before they would be discovered. At this point, some opposition members decided on a rescue. They knocked on the door, stating that they feared the building would be set afire. Smallwood picked up a long iron poker from the fireplace, vowing that if they brought him down he would take six with him. Lady Squires berated them for having fomented the riot. Appalled that she was in the room, the rescue team begged her to come out and she was finally escorted to safety.

Then Squires, disguising himself by removing his glasses and pulling his cap down low, was led out the door and might have made it to a car except that, not seeing too well, he tripped over a gate. The crowd spotted him and descended. The rescuers managed to get Squires across Military Road onto Colonial Street, a narrow street with square wooden houses tight against each other. The crowd surged after him. About a hundred yards down the street at number 66 stood the house of a Mrs. Connolly. She opened her door and Squires was pushed inside. Before the mob could follow, Reverend Father Joseph Pippy of St. Joseph's Parish, dressed in his clerical robes, stationed himself in the doorway with arms outstretched and barred the way. He probably saved Squires' life.

Squires was hustled through the house, out the back door, across the yard, over a fence and in the back door of the opposite house on Bannerman Street. He hurried out the front door of that house, climbed into a waiting car and was whisked away to safety.

Squires' resignation was inevitable. On June 11, Newfoundland elected Frederick C. Alderdice prime minister in a Conservative land slide.

a stern Scottish lawyer

The problems facing the Alderdice ministry were monumental. The country was still broke, with no way of paying the interest on its debts. Alderdice appealed for help to R.B. Bennett, to the banks and to the British government. He even tried to sell Labrador, all to no avail. On February 17, 1933, the British, Canadian and Newfoundland governments together set up a commission under the chairmanship of a stern Scottish lawyer, Wil-

Sir Richard Squires
PM Before the Fall

The man whose misfortune it was to be Newfoundland's prime minister during the early years of the '30s, Richard Squires was born in Harbour Grace in 1880. He entered politics at twenty-nine, two years before he was called to the bar, and was attorney general and Liberal leader between 1914 and 1923. Like many other politicians he ran into trouble during the Depression when he tried to appease the financial demands of big business and those who couldn't find a job. In April 1932 an angry mob 10,000 strong, incited by claims made by opposition whip Peter Cashin, pursued the PM through the streets, ransacked government offices, and would have killed the man had he not escaped through the assistance of a young man named Joey Smallwood.

E.J. Pratt
The Bard of Newfoundland
Everyone read poetry in the days when Canada's poet of the stormy sea, Edwin John Pratt was born in Western Bay, Nfld., 1883. The son of a Methodist minister, he was a teacher and preacher himself until he left the Island to go to university in 1907. His first book of verse, *Rachel* (1917), was a portrait of a mother awaiting news of her son who had drowned at sea, and throughout his long writing career he returned to the subjects of his youth. Ned Pratt was a poet of great wit and whimsy, though. His imaginative and incisive fables of the '20s and '30s express more about the human condition than a hundred tracts and pamphlets. His longer poems, *The Roosevelt and the Antinoe* (1930), *The Titanic* (1935), *Brébeuf and His Brethren* (1940), and *Towards the Last Spike* (1952), for which he is best known, won him the popularity he enjoyed in his lifetime and the reputation he has today.

liam W. Mackenzie, Baron Amulree, to investigate the problem and propose solutions.

Interestingly, the two Canadian members of the Commission wanted to bring Newfoundland into Confederation. The time was not ripe, however, and it would be thirteen years before this perennial proposal would surface again. What the Amulree Commission did decide was that Newfoundland should give up its responsible government and be ruled by a commission of six, three from Britain and three from Newfoundland including Alderdice, under the leadership of British Admiral Sir David M. Anderson. The deed was formally done on February 16, 1934, and England took over immediate responsibility for the country's interest payments, thus avoiding default.

"pauperism and starvation"

The commission proceeded to administer the country, introducing the efficient methods of the British civil service. It reorganized the various departments of government, reformed the post office and customs regulations, and revised the tariff system. One British member, Thomas Lodge, a discontented, arrogant, tactless and failed civil servant with a low opinion of Newfoundlanders, decided that the residents should abandon fishing and take up farming. Although the Newfoundland members opposed this motion vigorously, two land settlements were achieved, one at Markland in the interior of the Avalon Peninsula and the other at Winterland on the Burin Peninsula. Both were successful and today the bulk of Newfoundland potatoes come from Winterland.

In the meantime, the Depression continued. Clothing was in tatters, roofs leaked, tin cans served as cups, rusty cookie can lids for frying pans. Ordinary Newfoundlanders in the cities and outports drifted further and further into what the Amulree Commission described as "pauperism and starvation" while the merchants of St. John's went on in their accustomed luxury.

In a letter home one of the British commissioners, Sir John Hope Simpson, wrote:

It is remarkable to note the apparent prosperity of the mercantile community in St. John's, who live in luxury and seem to have money for everything they want. I was dining last night at the home of one of these merchants . . . I raised the problem of the fisherman. The three merchants were agreed that the standard of comfort was very low, but the fisherman wanted nothing more and was happy struggling along in the circumstances in which he found himself.

Sir John was warned by the merchants that the commission must do nothing to upset the class structure – a few rich and many poor – by raising the hopes of the poor.

By 1939 there were a record 58,187 people on relief each month and there is no telling what would have happened if the condition had continued. But it didn't. During World War II, the island's location made it vitally important in the trans-Atlantic war effort. The Americans and British moved in with airforce and naval bases, the price of fish went up and men became important again.

Newfoundlanders had lost control of their country, however, never to be regained, and for a proud and independent people this was the most devastating result of the Dirty Thirties.

Bluenose Victory

The pride of Nova Scotians from the time she first raced in the twenties–the *Bluenose*. From 1921 to 1939 she dominated the world of international sailing.

Canada issued this stamp commemorating the schooner's outstanding victories.

Captain Angus Walters, with the coveted Fisherman's Trophy his crew won in '38.

CHAPTER NINE

"We Mean Business"

You can't talk religion to a man who has had nothing to eat for three days.

William Aberhart

"We mean business!" the man on the platform shouted. He was large and his face flushed as he spoke. "People on the platform, what do you say?"

"We mean business!"

"Ladies in the audience, what do you say?"

"We mean business!"

"Men in the audience, what do you say?"

"We mean business!"

"All together, say it!"

"WE MEAN BUSINESS!"

"And I mean business! Tell your friends and neighbours when you meet them that Aberhart means business!"

Few Canadians stirred up more controversy, attracted more devotion or incited more hatred during the thirties than William Aberhart. Some people called him an emissary of God; others said he was a tool of the devil. Actually, he was a practical man of good morals and intentions, a teacher and a preacher, a rather shy and self-effacing man in private life. On the public platform or in front of a microphone, however, he was a rootin'-tootin' spellbinder of the old school. Almost single handedly William Aberhart founded a new and successful political party, became the first Social Credit Premier of Alberta and changed the voting patterns of the Canadian West.

William Aberhart was not the only politician borne of the Depression. In 1934, Ontario elected the most colourful and flamboyant leader that conservative province had ever seen. Mitchell Frederick Hepburn was an onion farmer and he spoke the farmers' language. "Our Mitch" called the millionaire Prime Minister Bennett, who owned the controlling interest in the E.B. Eddy Co., "Lord Matchbox." His quick and corny wit delighted the farmers and he hit the rural areas like a cyclone, drawing larger crowds than the Liberals had seen in decades, clowning, parodying and mercilessly castigating his opponents. He believed in the "big show." He met the people, talked with them, argued with them and swore with them, and the desperate farmers gave him their confidence. Hepburn carried the province in 1934 and became its first Liberal premier in almost thirty years.

At first the new premier lived up to his election promises. He passed legislation to protect farm prices and, at the same time, to safeguard the rights of trade unions. Like most other government leaders of the thirties, however, Hepburn became alarmed by the "agitators" among the unemployed and union ranks. His carefree and careless personal behaviour, his pragmatism and his sus-

WOULD A WORM STARVE BECAUSE—
the APPLE was TOO BIG?

If It Is Physically Possible It Must Be Economically Feasible

MUST men and women and little children go under-nourished BECAUSE there is too much to eat?

MUST they live in hovels and shacks BECAUSE there is an abundance of home building materials?

MUST they go cold BECAUSE there is so much coal and wood and fuel?

MUST they be ill-clad BECAUSE we can make all the clothes they need?

MUST they go ill-shod BECAUSE we have leather in abundance, and BECAUSE we can make ALL the shoes we are able to wear?

The parable of the worm and the apple, one of the many riddles that swept Aberhart and the Social Credit party into office in 1935.

***Opposite page:** Picnic speaking in 1936, "Bible Bill" Aberhart explains his curious new alphabet: A for Aberhart and Alberta under the gospel of Social Credit.*

Mitch Hepburn
The Man Who Would Be King

"Our Mitch" they called him, the jocular, irreverent, tobacco-farmer turned politician. Mitchell Hepburn was born in St. Thomas, Ont., in 1896. Self-educated beyond high school, he was a bank employee until WWI and military service. His political career began in 1926 when he was elected to the House of Commons as a populist MP for Western Ontario. After two terms of goading R.B.B. and the Tories, he contested the Ontario leadership and became its first Liberal premier in almost 30 years. His victory was decisive and anomalous, and his eight years as premier are still regarded with favour by some, ridicule by others. It is curious at least that the man whose cabinet piloted the pro-labour Industrial Standard Act in '34 should use all means to put down the union movement in Ontario just months later and court the leaders of big business until his retirement.

ceptibility to big men with big money eventually led him into the camp of big business – the very enemy that he had attacked so successfully in his pre-election speeches.

His true colours were revealed when he mobilized the Ontario Provincial Police, nicknamed "Hepburn's Hussars," to smash the United Auto Workers' drive to unionize the province's automobile factories. He finally locked swords with the cautious and cagey Mackenzie King, against whom no politician ever won a battle. It was the end of Hepburn's political career and, for more than a generation, the end of the Ontario Liberal party.

defender of the Catholic faith

In Quebec, Maurice Le Noblet Duplessis would be luckier in his political machinations. The Union Nationale party was founded in 1935 in protest against the unemployment and severe economic hardships resulting from the Depression. The next year, the party succeeded in ousting Quebec's forty-year-old Liberal government on a platform of extensive economic, social and electoral reform. Shortly after the election, Maurice Duplessis gained absolute control of the party.

He too attacked the corruption of the Liberal government. He too promised the farmers that he would end all their ills. Once elected he became the defender of the Catholic faith, the enemy of radicals and non-conformists, and a white knight who would save his people from Communism.

Duplessis quickly consolidated his political position, stepping hard on the toes of all who dared to oppose him. In 1937, he passed the notorious Padlock Law, by which he could close and padlock any premises where men gathered to further Communism. "Communism" meant anything that he decided was dangerous to him or his party. Although Duplessis was defeated at the polls in 1939, he would be returned to power in 1944 to hold undisputed and absolute control of Quebec until his death fifteen years later.

The political story of the decade, however, belongs to William Aberhart. He was born on a farm near Seaforth, Ontario, December 30, 1878, and raised strictly in the Presbyterian faith. He obtained his early education in small rural schools, then continued to normal school and studied for a Bachelor of Arts degree through correspondence courses. During his student years he could never quite make up his mind whether to become a teacher or a preacher, and so he finally became both.

Aberhart went to Calgary in 1910. Teaching alone could not begin to use up his tremendous energies, however, and at night and on Sundays he taught a Bible Class. In 1927 he organized the Calgary Prophetic Bible Institute. His first student was a young, lean Saskatchewan boy named Ernest Manning. Manning studied for three years and became the Institute's first graduate. After that he never left Aberhart's side.

no-nonsense fundamental religion

With the advent of radio Aberhart realized that he could reach hundreds of thousands of listeners and he used it to the fullest extent. Financed by donations from his listeners, he began regular Sunday afternoon broadcasts in which he preached good, old fashioned, down-to-earth, no-nonsense fundamental religion. He was one of the first of the radio evangelists so plentiful during the thirties, and he was certainly one of the most powerful.

He came to the people of Alberta when they were most vulnerable, beaten down by Depression, disillusioned, frightened and confused. As one desperately poor farmer expressed it: "When things are hopeless, your mind goes back to

Protest Meeting

Tuesday, May 25th

7 P.M.

QUEEN'S PARK

SUBJECT:

Save Democracy in Ontario!

Against Hepburn's Anti-Labor Policies!

SPEAKERS—

Ald. Stewart Smith
Sam Scarlett
J. B. Salsberg

ALL WELCOME 5

For Ontario workers the love affair with Mitch Hepburn lasted only a year. In 1937 when auto workers in Oshawa tried to form a union, the premier ordered out the OPP. Labour and CCF leaders cried, "Fascist!"

One of the zanier events in the career of Ontario Premier Mitch Hepburn occurred at Varsity Stadium in '34. The fleet of 47 limousines bought by the former administration was auctioned off for $34,000.

Comic Propaganda

The Social Credit campaign of 1935 had its graphic moments. While cartoonists "outside the fold" penned satirical renderings of "Bible Bill" and the "new messiah," Major Douglas, Alberta Social Credit League artist Hansell used his graphic talents in a kind of illustrated sermon on the vices of Premier R.G. Reid, big eastern bosses and businesses, and the federal government. When the election was over, Albertans had embraced what the aging Stephen Leacock called, "certain profundities of British fog impossible for most people to understand which in sunny Alberta, by force of prayer, turned into Social Credit."

Resolved that,—To continue will get no results. (Agreed)

GIVE DOUGLAS A CHANCE

"NO MORE WOLVES AT THE DOOR"

The Solution of the Present Problem
"Purchasing power in the hands of the Consumer"

Would the Canadian Constitution prevent us from solving our problems?

NOW and **THEN**
"Good and welfare should be supreme."

childhood and the simple scriptures. When Mr. Aberhart's voice came over the air with his scripture lesson, something clicked in our minds."

Aberhart taught the virtues of honesty, self-reliance, responsibility, moral behaviour and forbearance, quoting the scriptures endlessly to back up his arguments. Ernest Manning was always at his side, helping with the broadcasts, leading the prayers, conducting the singing, exhorting the listeners to send in more money.

world-wide conspiracy of bankers

Everything might have continued this way, with Aberhart doing little more than urging people to turn to the Bible in their hour of need, if he had not happened to read a certain book. It was called *Social Credit, Unemployment or War,* and it was written by an Englishman named Maurice Colborne.

The book outlined the economic theories of a Scottish engineer named Major Clifford Hugh Douglas. It pointed out that the trouble with the economic world was that there was never enough money or credit to buy the goods available. Since price was made up of wages plus interest on money plus profit, there was never enough money in the wage envelope alone to pay it. This vicious system, Douglas maintained, was created and perpetuated by a world-wide conspiracy of bankers. Political parties, he said, were merely the tools of the bankers.

Aberhart borrowed the book from a friend while he was marking examination papers in Edmonton during the summer of 1932. His direct, mathematical mind seized on the salient points and believed it was a divine revelation. God had shown the way to rescue the people from the worst Depression of all time and it was up to him to spread the divine word.

The Social Credit doctrine according to Aberhart, had three basic components – the Cultural Heritage, the Basic Dividend and the Unearned Increment.

The Cultural Heritage was the stake that every bona fide citizen had in the wealth of the province. Aberhart estimated Alberta's total potential wealth at $2,406 million, which gave each citizen a share of $3,518.

Each bona fide citizen would be issued a certificate, which was as good as money, with which to buy food, shelter, and clothing. This was the Basic Dividend. Each citizen would get this over and above any salary he or she might be earning. The figures proposed were $25 a month for each adult over twenty-one years of age, $20 for those age twenty, $15 for those age nineteen, $10 for ages seventeen and eighteen and $5 per month for children from one year to sixteen.

no more degrading dole

To most Albertan families, many of whom had no cash money at all, the idea was wildly attractive. A family of eight, for example, could collect more than $100 a month. There would be no more relief and no more degrading dole, Aberhart said. Each person would merely be getting what he was entitled to. The certificate had to be spent; it could not be loaned or invested. If there was anything left over at the end of the year it could be used to buy Alberta bonds.

In the event that a farmer, businessman or any other citizen might get money through an increase in the value of land or stocks that he owned, Aberhart proposed that the government would tax away this money, because it required no work and was unearned. This aspect of the scheme did not bother the average Albertan, because nothing was increasing in value. So far as he or she could see, the plan had a lot more to give than to take away.

Aberhart brought his great teaching skill, or-

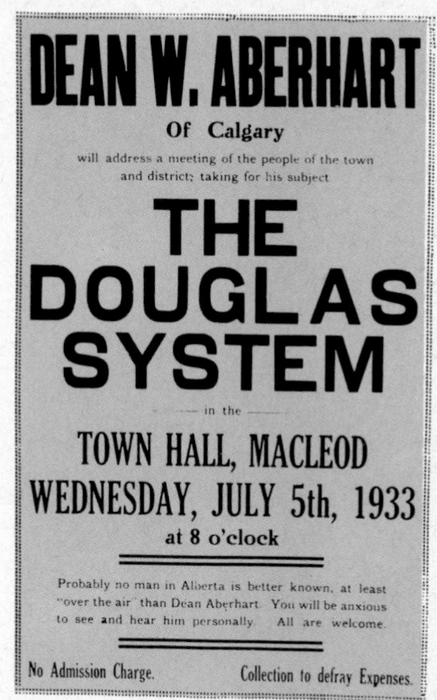

Certainly no man was better known to Alberta radio-listeners than Dean William Aberhart. By '33 the dynamic preacher and director of the Calgary Prophetic Bible Institute was touring the province proclaiming the gospel of British Utopian, C.H. Douglas.

Maurice Duplessis
"The Little Dictator"

Ruthless, cynical and totalitarian, Maurice LeNoblet Duplessis was a man of many faces. Born in 1890 in Trois Rivières, he began to flaunt his political views while most of his seminary classmates were still playing hockey. In 1913 he graduated in law from Laval, and by 1927, the year he was elected to Assembly, he was already known for his "fire and jest" oratory. When the monolith of L.A. Taschereau's Liberal government cracked in '35, Duplessis aligned himself with the rebels. The election the following year was a landslide for the Union Nationale coalition. Within days of his victory, however, *Le Chef* began to weed out opponents, replacing them with puppets whose strings he could easily control. His repressive Padlock Law and vigorous use of the QPP effectively smothered dissent among journalists, radicals and critics. Vote-buying, kick-backs and wholesale abuse of power were the means he used to achieve his so-called political aims. In 1939 he misjudged Quebeckers' commitment to the war effort, but he returned to office in '44 and ruled as before until his death in September 1959.

ganizational ability and oratorical powers to bear on expounding the Social Credit doctrine. He used diagrams, pamphlets, folk songs, humour, sarcasm – he was a master of them all. Everywhere he went he took his teaching aids, including immense coloured charts. One of these showed the bloodstream of credit compared with the bloodstream of the body. The flow must be uninterrupted and steady.

One favourite platform stunt was to stand before a live audience in a coat completely covered with old patches. It represented, he said, the old, worn-out, economic theories. As he expounded the virtues of Social Credit, his voice rising and his round face flushing, he ripped off the patches one by one and hurled them aside. Finally he stood there in a new, well tailored, modern coat. "This," he thundered, "is Social Credit!" It brought down the house.

swept like a prairie fire

William Aberhart was not a politician. His goal was to convince enough people of the truth of Social Credit that he could force one of the political parties to adopt his plan. He tried this with the governing United Farmers of Alberta party. He appeared before their convention and answered questions for them, but they took no action. He had no more success with the Liberals or Conservatives. They all tended to look upon him as a crackpot.

William Aberhart was being forced into politics. The tide of feeling he had begun in the province had swelled to a great wave. His disciples were mostly school teachers, preachers and farmers, given to the same oversimplification as he himself, but his organization was magnificent. He did not campaign, he taught. The province was organized into study groups – as many as 1,600 at the peak – and classes were conducted in schoolhouses, town halls and church basements. They were always packed. People came from ten, twenty miles in Bennett Buggies, jalopies, cutters or on horseback. Many trudged through the snow in below zero weather.

A provincial election had been called for August 22, 1935. With incredible speed, the new party nominated a candidate for each of the sixty-three ridings, many of them Aberhart's personal choices. The local meetings increased. The lessons became more convincing. The radio thundered the message. The voters came out 300,000 strong, a far greater percentage of those eligible than had ever before voted in Alberta. When the votes were all counted, the new party had swept like a prairie fire across the province and elected fifty-six members.

Aberhart himself had not been a candidate, but a seat was soon found for him in the Okotoks-High River riding. On September 3, 1935, he was sworn in as premier of Alberta.

As an evangelist and teacher he could talk and persuade and convince. Now he was the head of a government with a tremendous debt to be paid and civil service salaries to be met, and neither he nor any of his fifty-six members had ever sat in a legislature before. In addition, there were powerful forces working against him.

ridiculed every joke

Until the day of the election, newspaper editors outside Alberta had no more interest in Aberhart than they had in any other evangelist. When he became head of the first Social Credit government in the world, however, he was news. In no time Edmonton was full of reporters who watched the premier's every move, recorded every gesture, analyzed every comment, and ridiculed every joke.

In his office in the Parliament Building, the new premier worked tirelessly. He had always considered education due for reform, and he appointed himself Minister of Education. He passed legislation to ease the burden of debt on the farmers, and he hired a financial expert to advise him on the best means of cleaning up the mess left by the previous government. Social Credit, he decided, must be introduced gradually.

Here he learned his first devastating lesson. To the voters, an election promise is an election promise, and they wanted their money. In their jubilation over the election, farm wives pored over the mail order catalogues picking out the things they would buy with their share of the cultural heritage. Some quit their jobs, convinced they could now try something more compatible.

". . . the engagement is off!"

Aberhart reminded his people that he had specifically stated that no dividends would be paid for eighteen months. He was not used to making excuses, or explaining, and he didn't know how to placate. His relations with the reporters were abominable. He scolded them and called them "creatures with mental hydrophobia." Speaking on the national radio network, he stated ruefully that he felt like the young woman who, in the throes of having a baby, cried out, "If this is what marriage is like, you can tell my young man the engagement is off!"

Some of the new government members, alarmed by the unrest in their constituencies, began to demand action from their boss. Some even held clandestine meetings in the basement of the Corona Hotel and talked openly of dumping the chief. When finally, in January of 1937, after months of hard work, a sound orthodox budget was brought down calling for over $1 million in increased taxes, the howl from the people, the editors, and the insurgent members was heard across Canada.

Funny Money

One of the Utopian schemes of the Aberhart government was the creation of provincial "Prosperity Certificates"–commonly called "funny money." $360,000 of scrips were issued and used to pay for goods and services. Merchants affixed a 1¢ tax stamp on receipt to eventually cover their value.

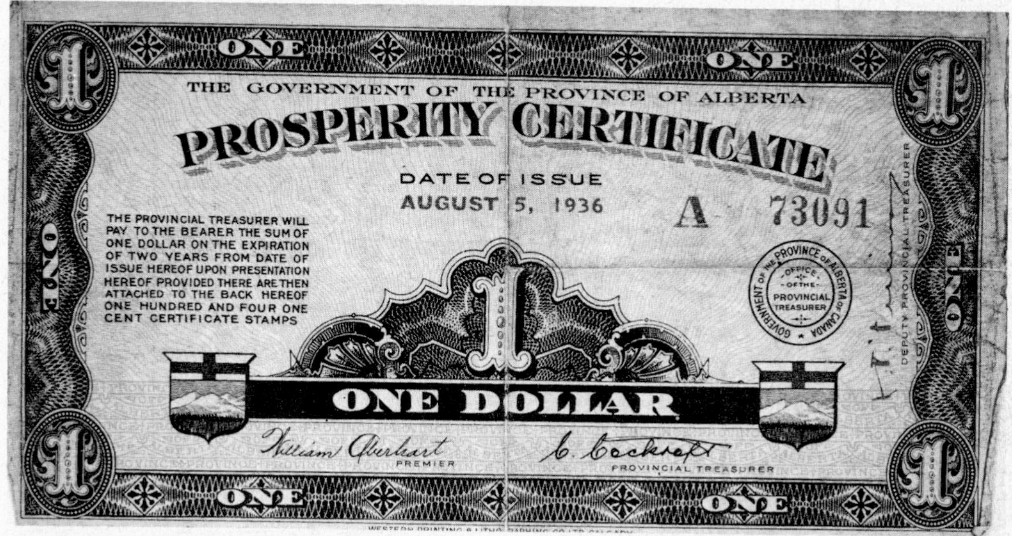

210

ALBERTA 1 CENT	ALBERTA 1 CENT	ALBERTA 1 CENT	ALBERTA 1 CENT	ALBERTA 1 CENT	ALBERTA 1 CENT	SEPT. 23. 1936	SEPT. 30. 1936	OCT. 7. 1936	OCT. 14. 1936	OCT. 21. 1936	OCT. 28. 1936	NOV. 4. 1936	NOV. 12. 1936	NOV. 18. 1936
NOV. 25. 1936	DEC. 2. 1936	DEC. 9. 1936	DEC. 16. 1936	DEC. 23. 1936	DEC. 30. 1936	JAN. 6. 1937	JAN. 13. 1937	JAN. 20. 1937	JAN. 27. 1937	FEB. 3. 1937	FEB. 10. 1937	FEB. 17. 1937	FEB. 24. 1937	MAR. 3. 1937
MAR. 10. 1937	MAR. 17. 1937	MAR. 24. 1937	MAR. 31. 1937	APRIL 7. 1937	APRIL 14. 1937	APRIL 21. 1937	APRIL 28. 1937	MAY 5. 1937	MAY 12. 1937	MAY 19. 1937	MAY 26. 1937	JUNE 2. 1937	JUNE 9. 1937	JUNE 16. 1937
JUNE 23. 1937	JUNE 30. 1937	JULY 7. 1937	JULY 14. 1937	JULY 21. 1937	JULY 28. 1937	AUG. 4. 1937	AUG. 11. 1937	AUG. 18. 1937	AUG. 25. 1937	SEPT. 1. 1937	SEPT. 8. 1937	SEPT. 15. 1937	SEPT. 22. 1937	SEPT. 29. 1937
OCT. 6. 1937	OCT. 13. 1937	OCT. 20. 1937	OCT. 27. 1937	NOV. 3. 1937	NOV. 10. 1937	NOV. 17. 1937	NOV. 24. 1937	DEC. 1. 1937	DEC. 8. 1937	DEC. 15. 1937	DEC. 22. 1937	DEC. 29. 1937	JAN. 5. 1938	JAN. 12. 1938
JAN. 19. 1938	JAN. 26. 1938	FEB. 2. 1938	FEB. 9. 1938	FEB. 16. 1938	FEB. 23. 1938	MAR. 2. 1938	MAR. 9. 1938	MAR. 16. 1938	MAR. 23. 1938	MAR. 30. 1938	APRIL 6. 1938	APRIL 13. 1938	APRIL 20. 1938	APRIL 27. 1938
MAY 4. 1938	MAY 11. 1938	MAY 18. 1938	MAY 25. 1938	JUNE 1. 1938	JUNE 8. 1938	JUNE 15. 1938	JUNE 22. 1938	JUNE 29. 1938	JULY 6. 1938	JULY 13. 1938	JULY 20. 1938	JULY 27. 1938	AUG. 3. 1938	

The cornucopia of the Canadian West, a 1937 view from Ottawa. The gradual economic recovery prompted eastern manufacturers to look to the Prairies for a market for industrial goods.

Aberhart found himself in the middle of his own prairie fire and he got badly burned. He was accused of betraying the voters, double-crossing the caucus, and financing the government on "the pennies of the poor." Out-of-town reporters made the most of his misery, reporting to the world that Social Credit was a dismal failure.

In 1937, Aberhart set up a Social Credit Board, chaired by insurgent Glen Maclachlan, with power to go ahead and introduce Social Credit by the quickest means possible. In the parliamentary session beginning August of the same year, the Board came out fighting. In three days the legislature passed three bills controlling banking in Alberta. Within a short time the federal government, acting through the Governor General, Lord Tweedsmuir, ruled that the three acts were contrary to the Canadian Constitution.

Aberhart accused the financially powerful and industrial East of stepping in to prevent an honest attempt by Alberta to improve itself. "Those plotters, those money barons, those sons of Satan – they shall not oppose the will of the people of Alberta!" he roared.

Now the people were with their prophet again. The real enemy had been identified. The wrath that had accumulated over the years because of high tariffs that prevented them from buying cheaper in the United States, banks that would not lend them money, implement companies that reclaimed their farm machinery, wheat speculators and Bay Street manipulators – it all burst forth. The people stood like rocks behind their leaders.

Bolstered by this support, the Alberta legislature held another special session and re-stated its position. The controversial bank-licensing bills were re-enacted and another bill was passed imposing heavy taxes on the banks.

Goaded by what they considered to be irresponsible reporting by the press, the legislature passed the Accurate News and Information Act, which stipulated, in effect, that newspapers had to print what the Social Credit Board told them to print. This only served to increase the animosity of the newspapers, from the powerful Edmonton *Journal* to the lowliest weekly in the province. The *Journal* won the prestigious Pulitzer Prize for its part in the fight against the act.

No one was actually arrested or punished under what was popularly known as the "Press Gag Act," although there was a threat to send one reporter to jail. The controversial legislation was fought all the way to the Supreme Court of Canada, which overturned it.

When Canada declared war in the fall of 1939, the fight between the province and the federal government ended. The war united the nation, put money into circulation, and ended the Depression in the West.

In the election of 1940 Aberhart was again in a strong position. His study groups were as powerful as ever. He broadcast every Sunday night from a public meeting in Edmonton, he and Ernest Manning, the man who upon Aberhart's death three years later, would become the second Social Credit premier of Alberta. Despite the fact that he had not given a basic dividend to one single person, his government was re-elected with thirty-six of the fifty-seven seats.

In many ways, William Aberhart *was* Social Credit. Without his zeal, energy, fanatical enthusiasm, organizational ability and persuasive power the movement never could have succeeded. Certainly this makes "Bible Bill" – whether one considers him as a sincere honest man or an "evangelistic racketeer," as he was described by one editor – one of the most colourful and important Canadians.

The Style for '33 ...and '38

Canada's love affair with the automobile, which began after the turn of the century, continued despite the Depression. Manufacturers in the '30s abandoned the boxy "twenties look" in '35 for "speed lines." The rumble seat disappeared and starting handles became only an emergency measure. By the end of the decade the automatic transmission revolutionized driving. Running boards got narrower, living room comfort and space became standard in interiors, and there was talk of radio in the streamlined '40s models.

Chatelaine, July, 1933 21

Vacationing?

HERE'S HOW TO GO FURTHER FOR LESS MONEY!

CHEVROLET

PRODUCED IN CANADA

GM GENERAL MOTORS PRODUCTS

WEEK-END jaunt or two-weeks' tour—either one quickly proves that you save with a new Chevrolet Six. Gasoline?—gallons s-t-r-e-t-c-h further in a Chevrolet than in the tank of any other full-size car. Oil?—put five quarts in the Chevrolet crankcase and the chances are those five quarts will still be there when you change your oil again. Repairs?—Chevrolet owners go thousands of miles without ever spending a penny. And the price you'll pay for the Chevrolet Standard Six is lower than that of *any* other full-size, six-cylinder closed car you can buy!

Think of the comfort and safety you'll enjoy—driving a new car with a big, roomy Fisher body, Fisher No-Draft Ventilation, safety glass windshield and syncro-mesh shifting. Think of the trouble you'll be spared — with new tires, new battery and an engine tuned to perfection. Think of the fun you'll have — going a greater distance than you ever planned, for less than you figured you'd spend! Does a holiday like that appeal to you? Then begin it today at your Chevrolet dealer's.

CHEVROLET

STANDARD SIX . . . . MASTER SIX

The new Fords for '38 with standard six or V-8 engine (85 hp!). Design with economy in mind, 22-27 miles per gallon.

The 1933 Chevrolet-traditional in style and elegant in design. This two-seater convertible sports the good, old rumble seat.

Ads & Jingles

The world of advertising in the '30s was a riot of brand names, gimmicks and jingles. New inventions, "improved" products, and unusual obsessions in the market required a more alluring pitch in tight-money days, and the ad industry rose to the occasion. Comic strip ads dramatized domestic disasters that would ensue if certain products were not taken seriously: household and personal cleanliness were just not possible using Brand X soap or lotion; Ipana invented "Irium" to combat "pink toothbrush," Fels-Naptha banished "tattle-tale grey," Palmolive Shave Cream (in a tube) promised a "quick, cool, smooth shave," and Lux was the only cure for "dish-pan hands." Refrigerators were the $125+ answer to the old ice box; food wrapped in "cellophane" appeared at the grocer's; canned soups and baby foods cut down "hovering-over-a-hot-stove time"; and aluminum, rayon and nylon were the scientific finds of the decade. Liquor was not advertised.

"Gingervating" Canada Dry – Oshawa druggist J.J. McLaughlin patented the recipe in the 1890s, but "The Champagne of Ginger Ales" didn't become popular until the prohibition years of the '20s.

Ottawa's Chateau Cheese Co. pitched its promo to the cost and nutrition conscious.

"Easy come, easy go" ads like this used Depression catch-phrases commercially.

Gold Flakes, Turrets and Winchesters – popular with smokers in the thirties.

Oxydol's colour comic catches poor Stella Payne at pre-washing-machine drudgery.

The 27¢ price, the 78 rpm record player and the fashions give away this ad's date

A tenuous relation between the product and the "cigar store Indian" is in fine print.

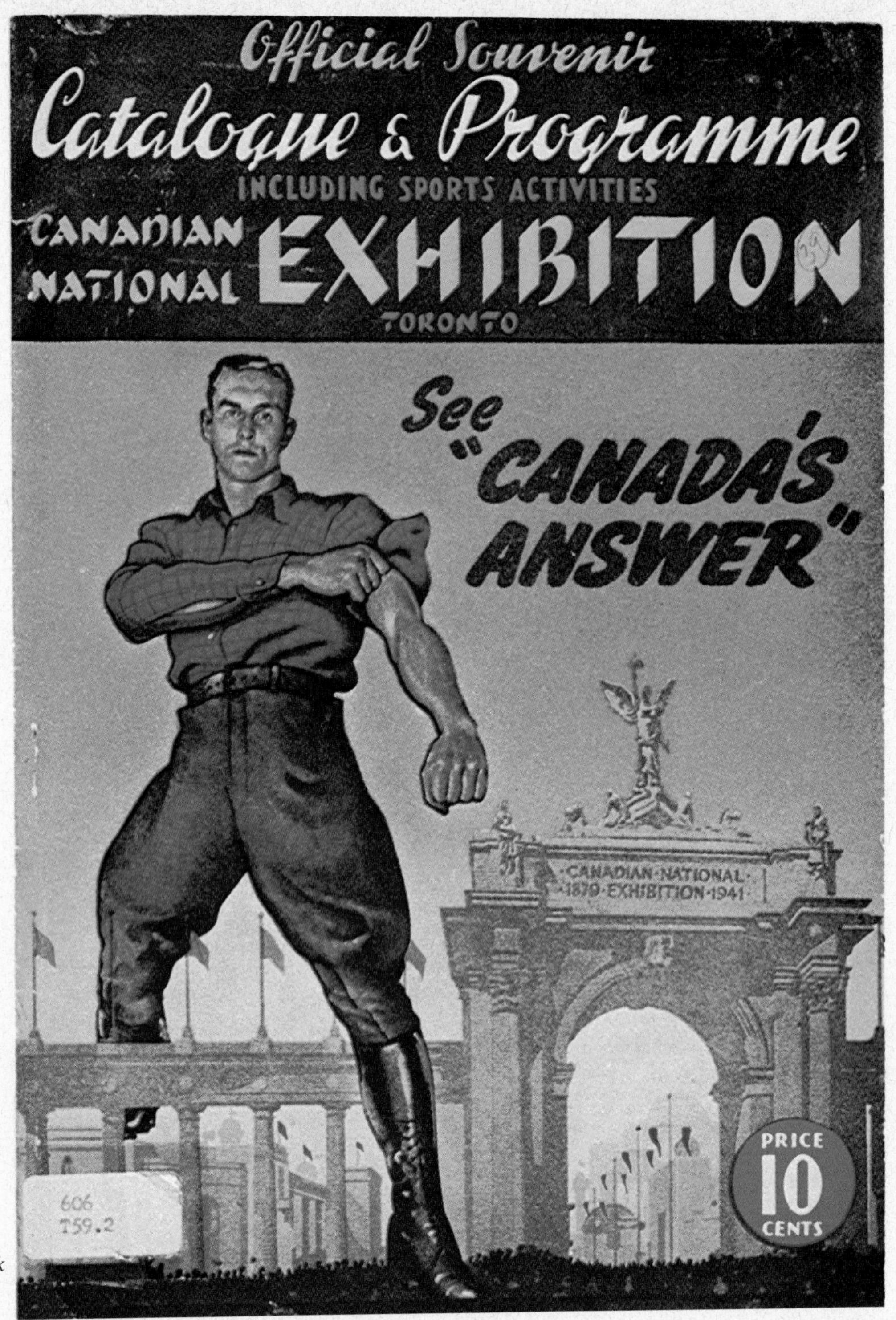

In 1939 Canada's answer to the outbreak of WW II was to roll up its sleeves. Most thought of it as "a phony war."

CHAPTER TEN

A Long Way Across the Atlantic

Hitler . . . will rank someday with Joan of Arc among the deliverers of his people.

Prime Minister Mackenzie King, after meeting with German dictator, 1938

The thirties was a decade of demagogues. While Canada had some relatively peaceful ones, those in other countries led their people and the world into World War II. Perhaps it could not have happened the way it did without the radio, for while the demagogues of the past found it difficult to reach a thousand people at a time, those of the thirties used this new communications medium to reach millions with one shout.

In Japan the war leaders filled people's minds with the conviction that China blocked their prosperity, and in 1931 led them into an invasion of Manchuria. In Germany, Adolf Hitler used the radio to convince millions that hatred and bigotry would save the country. In Italy, a pompous and posturing Mussolini roared through the radio that the country's salvation lay in the destruction of Ethiopia. In Russia, Joseph Stalin controlled all communications, including radio, to subjugate that country's population.

Canadians heard what was going on but paid little attention. They had troubles enough at home they thought – farms that blew away, unemployment, riots, even starvation. When they did turn on the radio it was to forget these troubles, to laugh at Joe Penner or dance to Benny Goodman. The cute antics of the Quints at their second birthday party made better listening than the sombre account of Hitler's re-occupation of the Rhineland.

Occasionally, of course, Canadians were forced to pay attention. One newsreel shot of a Japanese soldier pinning a Chinese baby to a door with his bayonet made some Canadians so sick they had to leave the theatre. But it did not start any concerted demonstrations against the shipment of Canadian scrap iron to Japan. A poetic account by Mussolini's famous aviator son telling how, when his bombs hit them, the tribesmen of Abyssinia "rose like the opening petals of a flower," offended most people, but failed to precipitate any mass clamour for stronger action by the League of Nations.

It is doubtful if a more noble experiment in human relations ever died a more ignoble death than did the League of Nations in the thirties. The effort to substitute reason and discussion for bullets and bombs in the settling of world affairs withered away without more than a handful of Canadians knowing or caring that it was dying.

Many Canadians were not convinced that Hitler himself was such an evil fellow. *Maclean's* magazine published an article on July 1, 1935, titled "The Germany I Saw" which recorded the impressions of a visiting Canadian businessman: "Everyone seems to be busy in Germany . . . . A dictatorship may have its drawbacks, but it at least

Maclean's *streetcar ad for Mar. 1, 1939 posed a question of growing concern for all Canadians.*

Dr. Norman Bethune
A Hero in Another Country

Who would have thought in 1890 that a boy from Gravenhurst, Ont., would become one of the most revered men in China? With the outbreak of war in 1914, Bethune left his medical studies and was one of the first 10 men to enlist. Wounded at Ypres in a valiant rescue, he spent months recovering, returned to the U. of T. for his degree, then rejoined the military. In the post-war years his practice took him to the slums of Detroit, but the long hours and hard life caught up with him and in 1929 he was confined to hospital, dying of pulmonary TB. An untried surgical experiment saved his life, and he returned to Canada to become one of the world's most respected MDs. The Civil War in Spain drew Bethune once again into the battle zone. He created the first mobile blood unit ever used in war. Outspoken in his anti-fascism, he returned home with horror stories that few would believe. Disillusioned with democracy, he went to China in 1938 as a medic to aid in the war against fascist Japan. It was there he died in Nov. 1939, a patriot to an adopted country.

has power and this has been used in Germany to see that everyone is occupied!" He went on to say that he did not consider there was any sentiment among the German people for war.

It's true that some of our leaders were alarmed. Senator and former prime minister Arthur Meighen, in a speech to the World Alliance for International Friendship, warned that "Man will destroy himself unless he gets rid of war by organizing for peace."

offend the strutting dictators

Other Canadians did more than talk. Deeply disturbed by the rise of dictatorship, some determined to fight for democracy wherever they saw that fight being waged. The Spanish Civil War, which broke out in 1936 between the socialist Popular Front and the Fascists led by General Francisco Franco, involved Canadian leftists along with those from the United States and Britain. Canadians joined the Mackenzie-Papineau Battalion of the International Brigade. Many died for their principles in Spain.

The most noted Canadian freedom-fighter was Dr. Norman Bethune of Gravenhurst, Ontario. A veteran of World War I, Bethune served in Spain with the Popular Front where he organized a blood transfusion service that saved thousands of lives. Later he joined the Chinese Communists in their struggle against Japanese aggression during the late thirties. Serving with the beleaguered Eighth Route Army, he literally worked himself to death in 1939.

Like most other democratic leaders of the thirties, both R.B. Bennett and Mackenzie King showed a great reluctance to say or do anything that might offend the strutting dictators of Japan, Germany, Italy and Spain. When Japan defied the League of Nations with her attack on Manchuria, the Bennett government failed to support the League with pledges of either men or money. In fact they had a definite policy against it.

When, during the Italy-Ethiopia crisis of 1935, Canada's representative to the League of Nations proposed that member nations refuse to sell oil to the aggressors – a move that might have stopped the aggression right there – he was slapped down by his boss, Mackenzie King himself, who felt that Canada should keep out of European squabbles.

Like many other leaders in the western world, King seemed to believe that if the crisis was not aggravated it would solve itself. And like the others, he was fooled by Hitler, whom he considered, after meeting him, to be a reasonable man. His principal concern was to keep both English and French Canadians in a frame of mind that would make it possible for Canada to support Britain if a showdown came.

". . . this country is at war . . . "

Right up until the early morning of September 3, 1939, many Canadians believed war would not happen. That morning they crawled sleepy-eyed out of bed and sat shivering in the chill September dawn as they listened to the voice of a broken and shattered man, who had jauntily boasted after his Munich meeting with Hitler that he had secured "peace in our time," admit that he had been unable to keep the country he loved out of war. "I am speaking to you from the cabinet room of Number 10 Downing Street," began British Prime Minister Neville Chamberlain. He related how the Germans, after attacking Poland, had ignored the Allied ultimatum, and ended with the statement, "and consequently this country is at war with Germany."

Across the country, Canadians crawled back into bed and stared in the dim light at the ceiling, trying to assess what changes the war would bring to their lives.

The World of Dr. Bethune

One of the world's great humanitarians, Dr. Norman Bethune saw the world of the thirties from a different viewpoint. When the Fascist forces of Europe over-ran war-torn Spain, he was on the battlefield (left) providing medical aid to the Loyalists. When Japan invaded China, he worked shoulder-to-shoulder with Chinese supply and medical officers (below) and became Mao's chief medic in 1939. The soldiers called him Pai Chu En, a term of great respect, and to this day his name is recognized by the Chinese as a hero.

Despite Mussolini's alliance with Fascist Germany, Canadian magazines carried tourism ads for the sunny Mediterranean as late as Mar. '39.

Next day came the broadcast message from King George VI who had visited them only last summer with his beautiful queen:

In this grave hour, perhaps the most fateful in our history, I send to every household of my peoples, both at home and overseas, this message, spoken with the same depth of feeling for each one of you as if I were able to cross your threshold and speak to you myself.

He went on to assure his listeners that they were fighting for the principles of settled peace, security, justice and liberty among nations, and he warned:

The task will be hard. There may be dark days ahead . . . war can no longer be confined to the battlefield; but we can only do the right as we see the right, and reverently commit our cause to God.

The speech of Mackenzie King was broadcast six days later, on September 10, when Canada formally declared war on Germany. He explained sombrely that the issue in the war was:

two diametrically opposed systems, the one believing in Christianity, the brotherhood of man, and the value of human personality, and the other on the pagan doctrine of might and power.

So Canada was at war, and rumours abounded. Remembering the shortages of World War I, many people rushed to the stores and bought sugar. One man bought a hundred pounds of flour, even though his wife seldom baked. Another short-lived rumour said that all marriages would be banned for the duration, and licence bureaus were swamped with desperate applicants.

War was exciting. Ministers preached about the sacred duty to rid the world of tyranny; editors wrote stern editorials about what the government should do; women's club members got in stacks of

Mackenzie King's Horoscope

William Lyon Mackenzie King, Canada's controversial prime minister, was also an ardent spiritualist. Before his return to office in 1935 and while he was leader of the Opposition in Commons, he delved into palmistry, automatic writing, occult phenomena and visited mediums. His diaries show at least two "successful" visits from the world beyond, one from his mother and the other from former PM Wilfrid Laurier.

King and his Irish terrier, Pat. He had great affection for the dog, and when it died he mourned it publicly.

Geraldine Cummins, one of Mackenzie King's spiritualists. When her advice led him astray, he tried to use reason.

SAGITTARIUS — The Archer

NOVEMBER 22nd TO DECEMBER 21st

Ruled by Jupiter

★

♃ ⟶ THESE people, like the Archer, seldom miss their mark when acting upon first impressions and are most sure to meet with loss and disappointments when following the advice of others instead of their own judgment. They are strong, honest, fearless and blunt; say what they think and often make enemies by doing so. Having great power of concentration, they do one thing at a time and do it well (unlike Gemini people who do many things at a time and tire of each in turn). Sagittarius people work with tireless energy and cannot bear to leave a task unfinished, others often marvel at the extent of their great energy. Being open and honest themselves, they dislike secrecy, trickery or deception in others; a confidence once lost can seldom, if ever, be restored. These people are thrifty and practise economy closely and are seldom without money; are odd in their ways which makes them very hard to understand.

If Mackenzie King had looked under his sign Sagittarius in Your Horoscope *for 1930, he would have read this.*

wool and began to knit; veterans reported to their old units and, with fire in their eyes, told their sons that now they too would know what it was like. Everybody had a purpose; everybody had a goal. Doubt was gone; indecision and vacillation dispelled. As the Prime Minister had said, the issue was clear. They were the bad guys; Canadians were the good guys. Those who did not believe it had the good sense to keep their mouths shut.

Orders poured into the steel companies; the price of fish rose dramatically, as did the price of wheat. Textile mills tooled up for the orders they knew would be coming, for the country would soon need everything – trucks, planes, uniforms, boots, ships. Men who had not worked for years were hired at good wages. The war boom was on. If you enlisted you not only got paid, there was also an allowance for your wife and kids.

they had been bums

The greatest beneficiaries were the single, unemployed males. Yesterday they had been bums, Communists and rabble-rousers; today they were the defenders of democracy. Yesterday they could not get a job or a haircut; they did not have clothes, a decent meal or a roof over their heads. When they enlisted, they had two or three uniforms, sturdy boots, a warm bed every night, good pay and free dental and medical care.

Young men from the towns and farms poured into the cities to enlist – not by freight trains now, but first class. Everywhere public buildings were hastily converted into recruiting stations. Armouries could not hold the rush of recruits. In Toronto the immense horse palace on the Canadian National Exhibition grounds became an army barracks, full of naked men, clutching a file in their hands, waiting for a medical, waiting for a test, waiting for an interview.

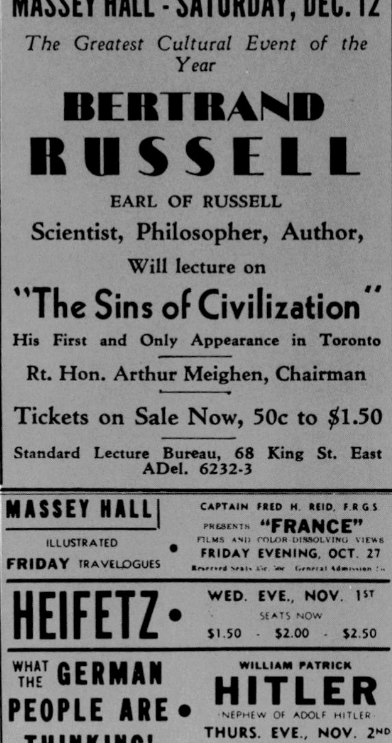

Entertainment at Toronto's Massey Hall in the thirties had its hours of greatness and moments of infamy. In 1930, the legendary Bertrand Russell lectured on "The Sins of Civilization"; in 1939 Hitler's nephew gave his views on "What the German People Are Thinking."

War!

Ready or not, on September 10, 1939, Canada was at war. The memory of the Great War was still fresh in people's minds, and the country was slow to mobilize. However, many did join up, especially those still unemployed.

CNE buildings at Toronto's Exhibition Park were converted into army and navy barracks (right). Recruitment officers gathered up enlistees and marched them off to camp (below).

Despite the soldiers who stood guard at strategic locations (left), the war seemed unreal at first. It became all too real when the First Division left for England from Halifax (below) in December 1939.

Cartoonists lampoon the waffling of King and Tory leader, Robert Manion.

—*Cartoon by Grassick.*

THE GENERALS: "Now, men, you decide where you want to go and, wherever it is, we are ready to follow."

The posh automotive building nearby became a naval "ship" where young men dressed in bell-bottomed trousers learned to march and tie knots and tell their starboard side from their port side. They picked up the salty jargon of the sea and listened bug-eyed to seasoned seamen and chief petty officers telling about the girls of Singapore and other glamour spots of the world.

"shipped out" to St. Hyacinthe

In Saskatoon the Navy rented an old garage on the corner of 1st Avenue and 25th Street and converted it into HMCS *Unicorn.* Naval ratings, some of them just past their seventeenth birthday, jaunty in their white caps and skin-tight jerseys, "came aboard" when they entered through the side door and "went ashore" when they left. Back home on leave, they beguiled family and friends with talk of being "shipped out" to St. Hyacinthe or Annapolis where they would be further trained for sea duty.

Prairie farm boys who had never seen a body of water bigger than a slough and had never been on a craft larger than a raft were anxious to join the navy and they made excellent sailors. The rigours of life on the prairies were much like those on the north Atlantic. The wind and sleet and ice of the sea was nothing new to a boy who had ridden perched on a load of poplar poles for ten miles through a thirty below blizzard.

The real glamour service was the air force. Since World War I, Canada had become a flying country. Hundreds of young men had been trained in the government-sponsored flying clubs and thousands more were keen to get into the air. Here was a place for the young men who had finished their high school education and then could not afford to go to university.

Not all the young men rushed to join the services, however. There were many who remembered books they had read and the talks they had had about peace. Books like *Merchants of Death* which maintained that wars were arranged by munitions manufacturers for profit; books that made a mockery of the World War I slogan "A war to save democracy." The sorry fate of the League of Nations had sorely disillusioned them. Writers like George Bernard Shaw, Bertrand Russell, Aldous Huxley and Upton Sinclair had etched into their minds the folly of all war. These young men fought hard against the rising militarism all about them.

Canada had become a military country. During the last four months of the decade preparations for the conflict were all about. To the city of Halifax war was an immediate thing. German submarines were known to be lurking in the Atlantic. As Canada's largest port on the European side, Halifax would be a prime target for saboteurs. The Nova Scotia Light and Power Company, essential to the operation of the port, was immediately protected by a new steel fence and round-the-clock supervision, and every precaution was taken with personnel and vehicles entering the plant.

10,000 men in the armed forces

Contracts were let for submarine nets to guard the harbour mouth; anti-aircraft batteries were installed; steel housings were built around the main electrical transformers to protect them from shell fragments. The city was full of sailors; activity was brisk in the harbour; and on Christmas 1939 no coloured lights were permitted on the houses or streets.

Like many of her allies, Canada was unprepared for war. There were fewer than 10,000 men in the armed forces. The guns available were out of date and there was a lack of ammunition, trucks, aircraft and just about everything needed for combat. At the moment of her declaration of war, Canada possessed exactly sixteen small tanks. The United States government made good use of the seven days during which Canada was nominally neutral, from September 3 to 10, to rush supplies across the border. Later, when Canada was at war, somebody devised a simple plan whereby the United States could supply aircraft without overtly violating its neutrality. Near Coutts, Alberta, a town which sits on the international boundary and is a port of entry for tourists, there was an airstrip right on the line. American planes were left a few feet from Canada, and Canadian airmen simply lassoed them and pulled them over. Thus Canada got some needed planes with no nationals illegally crossing the border.

cold grey face of disaster

The decade that began with a whimper ended with a bang. Canadians left behind them forever one of the most traumatic experiences of their lives. Many had stared into the cold grey face of disaster and would never forget the evil they saw there. They remembered animals dying in the fields for want of food, and children's bodies twisted and malformed for want of vitamins. They remembered Canadians rioting in the streets for bread, and other Canadians clubbing them over the head to make them stop.

The physical scars of the thirties were soon erased. The rain fell and the crops grew. The war took care of over-production and prices rose. Mental scars were not so easily healed. During the thirties, Canadians asked questions about their institutions, their economy, their laws, their government and even about Confederation itself. During and after the war, these questions would be asked again and again. The thirties lessened complacency in Canada, and timidity, and smugness. It may even have seen the real beginnings of Canada as a nation.

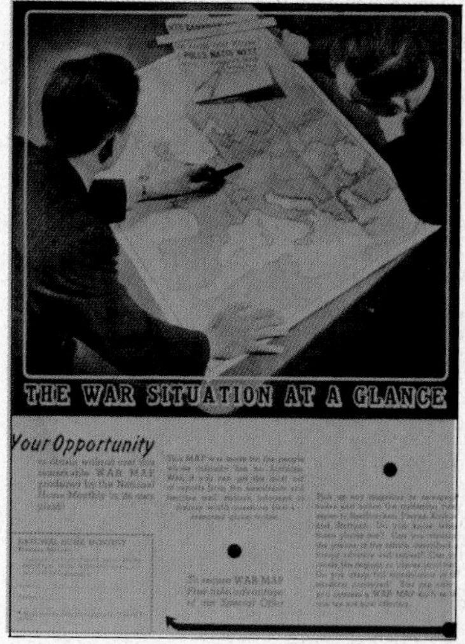

Readers of National Home Monthly *in December 1939 had a chance to see the war situation at a glance. In subsequent years the foreign place names became sadly familiar.*

Daily News & Sports

Strange, tragic, thrilling—the headlines of the '30s are a reflection of a brand of journalism in pre-TV days that ferreted out a good story as it was breaking. Some of the items that made the papers were…

1935: Bank robber "Red" Ryan is released from prison, a model of reform. He is shot months later in a hold-up.

1930: The British airship R-100 arrives at St. Hubert, Quebec, making the crossing in 78 hours and 52 minutes—the first and only trans-Atlantic airship to land in Canada.

1938: Niagara's 1,400 ft. Honeymoon Bridge collapses and plunges into the river. Miraculously no one is killed.

1936: Winnipeg inventor C.N. Pogue's 200-mile-per-gallon carburetor models are stolen from his workshop.

Their Invention Stolen by Thugs

Charles Nelson Pogue, inventor of the famous 200-miles-to-the-gallon carburetor, is seen seated in an auto equipped with his miraculous device which, some time Wednesday noon, was stolen from the Amphitheatre rink. Standing beside the car is W. J. Holmes, local business men, who has sponsored Mr. Pogue in perfecting his invention.

Thugs Raid C. N. Pogue's Workshop in Amphitheatre

Three Million-dollar Models of Device to Give Cars 200 Miles Per Gallon Are Stolen When Inventor Goes to Lunch

Police, Friday, are conducting a city-wide hunt for three "million-dollar carburetors," stolen from the inventor's workshop in the Amphitheatre rink some time during the noon hour Wednesday. Reputed to be capable of producing 200 miles to the gallon, when attached to standard makes of automobiles, theft of the carburetors wiped out the entire supply of the inventor, Charles Nelson Pogue.

Believed to have gained access to the building housing the workshop through the north door fronting on the Osborne stadium, the thieves showed a remarkable knowledge of the interior. Two men were seen scaling the north fence at Osborne stadium shortly after twelve o'clock, Wednesday, by employees of the adjacent brewery. They did not see them return.

How they entered the building remains a mystery, but once inside the thieves moved swiftly into action. Moving a small ladder against the side of the 10-foot workshop, they climbed to the roof and crossed over to southwest corner where, under the covering shavings they displaced an old trap-door, about two and a half feet in diameter. One thug dropped down inside the carefully locked workshop and the other remained on the roof.

Mr. Pogue left the workshop just before twelve. A watchman was in attendance near the front of the Amphitheatre rink proper. So swiftly and quietly did the determined thieves work, not an unusual sound was heard.

Theft Discovered

Mr. Pogue returned soon after 1 o'clock but did not detect the robbery until 3.30 o'clock. It was when he went to make an adjustment on the tank of the eight-sylinder car, the original trial automobile that he was amazed to find his invention of 18

Inventor

C. N. POGUE

Workings of Pogue's Mystery Carburetor Explained to Public

SIDE VIEW.

AIR INTAKE

CHOKE

SECONDARY MIXING CHAMBER

HEAT OUTLET

Inventor Regards Carburetor Theft As Foolish, Daring

C. N. Pogue and Sponsor of Device Declare They Will Not Be Deterred by Attempt to Defeat Their Plans

1932: Canadian Amateur Champ Sandy Somerville wins the U.S. amateur open and dominates golf throughout the decade.

1937: Montreal Canadiens star Howie Morenz (centre) dies of brain injuries sustained during a game. Sportswriters still pick him as one of the best there ever was.

1932: "Torchy" Peden wins the professional six-day bicycle races at New York's Madison Square Garden. Above, he takes one of the few spills he had in his illustrious career.

1939: Dorothy Walton wins the All-England Badminton Championships, outclassing all major competitors.

Acknowledgements

In addition to the written scholarship that exists on the Great Depression, the magazines and periodicals of the era were a great help in the preparation of this book. The Canadian Broadcasting Corporation's Archives were a valuable source of original material, especially for the history of Canadian radio and for the Aberhart era in Alberta.

But this book owes much to personal experience, both my own and the hundreds of people that I interviewed, people who lived through the period – merchants in St. John's, Newfoundland; farmers in Orangeville, Ontario, Saskatchewan townspeople in places like Eyre, Fielding, Aberdeen and Vonda. I especially want to thank Joey Smallwood who granted an extensive interview during my stay in St. John's.

Max Braithwaite

The Author

Max Braithwaite is one of Canada's best-known writers. He began his writing career during the hungry thirties while teaching school in his native Saskatchewan. After four years of active service, he was discharged in Toronto and continued his career there in radio, television and magazine writing.

He is the author of over twenty books, including *Land, Water and People, Never Sleep Three In A Bed, The Night We Stole the Mounties' Car, A Privilege and a Pleasure, The Western Plains,* and *Why Shoot the Teacher,* which became a motion picture in 1976. He now lives with his wife Aileen in Port Carling, Ontario.

Index

Picture Credits

We would like to acknowledge the help and cooperation of the directors and staff of the various public institutions and the private firms and individuals who made available paintings, posters, mementoes, collections and albums as well as photographs and gave us permission to reproduce them. Every effort has been made to identify and credit appropriately the sources of all illustrations used in this book. Any further information will be appreciated and acknowledged in subsequent editions.

The illustrations are listed in the order of their appearance on the page, left to right, top to bottom. Principal sources are credited under these abbreviations:

Glenbow-Alberta Institute Archives – GAF
Provincial Archives of Canada – PAC

/1 Private collection /2 All private collection, Photographer, Norman Mansfield /4 Confederation Life Insurance Company /6 Public Archives of Canada, C 27901 /7 London Life Insurance Company, London, Canada /8 National Home Monthly /9 Miller Services; Private collection /10 Jack V. Long /11 Private collection /12 Archives of Saskatchewan /13 Private collection /14 Provincial Archives of New Brunswick; Toronto Star; PAC C 30811 /15 Toronto Star; Mrs. H. Bain; Vancouver Public Library, 12748 /16 PAC C 47404; PAC C 47403 /17 PAC C 20013; PAC PA 35132; Saskatchewan Archives Photograph /18 Alexandra Archives; Mr. and Mrs. C. Jessop, Photograph by M. Hunter; McLean-Hunter #8806 /19 Canadian Pacific /20 GAF /21 National Home Monthly, Winnipeg; Maclean's; Proctor and Gamble Co. Ltd.; Private collection; Private collection; Bovril (Canada) Limited /22 All private collection /23 McLean-Hunter Limited; Liberty Magazine; Chatelaine /24 Charles Comfort, O.C., LL. D., and Hart House /25 GAF NA-3170-1 /26 Saskatchewan Archives A 613(8); GAF NA 2629-7 /27 Saskatchewan Archives A 613(3); William W. Smith /28 GAF 12955-F; GAF NA 2434-1 /29 Mrs. H. Bain; Dree-Pfra Photograph; GAF A 6343 /30 GAF /31 GAF NA 2237-1; GAF NA 2238-2 /32 Miller Services /33 National Gallery of Canada, Photographer, John Evans /34 Art Gallery of Ontario, Bequest of Charles S. Band, 1970; Credit artist's collection; Private collection /35 Collection of Mr. and Mrs. R. W. Finlayson /36 Alexandra Archives /37 Reproduction Courtesy Archives of Ontario /38 Jock Carrol /39 Provincial Archives of Manitoba; Reprint by permission of the Winnipeg Free Press; Winnipeg Free Press /40 Vancouver Public Library 8799; Toronto Star /41 Vancouver Public Library 8793; Star Photo Studio; McClelland and Stewart /42 Toronto Star /43 Archives of Saskatchewan A 7866 /44 PAC C 62100 /45 Archives, Eaton's of Canada, Limited /46 All Callander Museum /47 Robbins Music Corp., New York; The Canada Starch Company Limited; Callander Museum /48 Private collection /49 McClelland and Stewart /50 Toronto Telegram /51 Reprint through courtesy of Metropolitan Life Insurance Company /52 Empress Hotel; CBC; Canada Wide /53 North Bay Nugget /54 The LIFE SAVERS and LIFE SAVERS CONFIGURATION trademarks for Roll Candy are used by permission of Life Savers, Ltd. /55 Andrew C. Martin; Public Archives of Ontario 5801 /56 Courtesy of Mrs. J. de Roux, Photographer, Randolph Macdonald /57 Port Arthur News-Chronicle; Toronto Globe; The Portage la Prairie Daily Graphic /58 Courtesy of National Museum of Science and Technology, Ottawa, Canada /59 Canadian Airways /60 Courtesy of National Museum of Science and Technology /61 Courtesy of National Museum of Science and Technology, Ottawa, Canada; PAC C 57535 /62 Public Archives of Ontario 314255; Public Archives of Ontario S 14608; PAC C 28195 /63 GAF NA 1258-114; GAF NA 1258-106; GAF NA 1258-119 /64 Air Canada /65 All Canadian Pacific /66-67 National Home Monthly /68 Courtesy of Elwood Glover /69 Private collection /70 Private collection /71 Private collection /72 Courtesy of Elwood Glover; Maclean's /72-73 Courtesy of Elwood Glover /73 Penguin Photo; Private collection; The Museum of Modern Art; All rest courtesy of Elwood Glover /74 Canada Wide 001; Archives of Ontario; Provincial Archives of Manitoba, Foote collection /75 Imperial Tobacco /76 Private collection /77 Private collection /78 Ruth Lowe; Private collection /78-79 Canadian Music Sales Corp. Ltd. /79 Canadian Music Sales Corp. Ltd.; Shapiro, Bernstein and Co. Inc. /80 CBC /81 Courtesy of the Public Archives of Nova Scotia /82 CBC; Nova Scotia Museum /83 Courtesy of Gordon Sinclair /84 Alexandra Archives /86 Mr. G. Wilson; Sandy Stewart /87 All Sandy Stewart /88 The Calgary Herald /89 Toronto Public Library; Angelo Savelli; Bank of Toronto /90-91 Dominion Simplicity Patterns Ltd. /92 Photo courtesy of Newfoundland Archives /93 Department of Fisheries, Ottawa /94 Metropolitan Toronto Central Library /95 All Photo's courtesy of Newfoundland Archives /96 All Photo's courtesy of Newfoundland Archives /98 McClelland and Stewart /99 From the MacAskill Collection, Courtesy Sea and Sail Art Productions Limited, Halifax, Nova Scotia; PO2 Eugene Hovey, R.C.N.; From the MacAskill Collection, Courtesy Sea and Sail Art Productions Limited, Halifax, Nova Scotia /100 GAF NB 16-207; Private collection /102 Public Archives of Ontario S 323 /103 The Globe and Mail, Toronto; Private collection /104 Social Credit Assn. of Canada /105 The Globe and Mail, Toronto /106 GAF P-1223-2 /107 GAF NA 2377-1; GAF /109 General Motors of Canada, Ltd.; Ford Motor Company of Canada Ltd., Oakville, Ontario /110 Canada Dry Limited /111 Campbell Soup Co. Ltd.; The Proctor & Gamble Company of Canada, Limited; Courtesy of Coca-Cola Ltd., Toronto; Imperial Tobacco; Private collection; Private collection /112 MTCL, CNE /113 Maclean's /114 CBC /115 All CBC /116 Italian Line Ltd.; Private collection; National Film Board /117 McClelland and Stewart; Massey Hall /118 All The Toronto Telegram /119 Notman Photographic Archives MP 072; Reproduced by permission of the Minister of Supply and Services Canada, PAC C 14458 /120 Reprinted by permission of Winnipeg Free Press; Financial Post /121 National Home Monthly /122 Maclean's; Courtesy of National Museum of Science and Technology, Ottawa, Canada A 1151; Private collection; Reprinted by permission of the Winnipeg Free Press /123 Alexandra Studios; Canada Wide; Alexandra Studios; Private collection.

1935

Lord Tweedsmuir (John Buchan) becomes governor general.

The rumba becomes a popular dance.

Winnipeg Blue Bombers win first Grey Cup for the West.

HANSON STARTLES EAST; HAMILTON BEATEN 18 TO 12

Citizens Go Wild Over Win

Daily Woes Forgotten as They Celebrate Rugby Victory

Sensational Winnipegs Running Halfback Brings 9,000 Fans to Foot When Running 75 Yards for Touch-down—Title in West for First Time.

By ELMER DULMAGE.
Canadian Press Staff Writer.

Hamilton, Ont., Dec. 9 (CP)—Canadian football supremacy was en route west today, held by the Blue Warriors of Winnipeg, the one western team in history that smashed out triumph on an eastern gridiron. Winnipegs upset Hamilton Tigers in the inter-sectional final here Saturday 18-12.

While 9,000 wild-eyed spectators roared in a frenzy of excitement, the Blue challengers held off a desperate last-minute

W.R. Riddell proposes further League of Nations sanctions against Italy for aggression.

William Aberhart's Social Credit Party wins landslide victory in Alberta.

Quebec's Union Nationale Party is formed.

Liberal landslide in election returns Mackenzie King as PM.

"Reformed" bank robber "Red" Ryan is killed in Sarnia liquor store shootout.

Dorothea Palmer is arrested for distributing birth control information in Eastview, Ont.

Jazz goes "swing."

Toronto's Ada MacKenzie wins Canadian Open and Closed Golf Tournaments.

Relief camp strikers clash with police in Dominion Day riots in Regina.

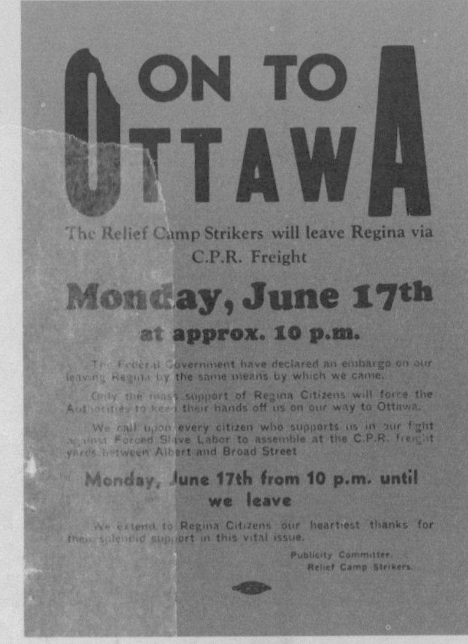

1936

Mt Waddington (13,200 ft.) in B.C. is climbed for the first time.

Supreme Court nullifies most of Bennett "New Deal."

Civil War breaks out in Spain. Canadians enlist to fight against Franco.

Canadian Grand Opera Assoc. begins premiere season at Toronto's Massey Hall.

Francis Amyot wins canoeing gold medal at Berlin Olympics.

Canadian Poetry Magazine publishes first issue.

Curler Ken Watson wins Brier and Manitoba Bonspiel.

CRBC is renamed Canadian Broadcasting Corporation.

B.C. becomes first province to legislate medical insurance.

Maurice Duplessis becomes Prime Minister of Quebec.

King George V dies, succeeded by Edward VIII.

Canadian Civil Liberties Union is founded.

THE PADLOCK ACT

has been held constitutional by the Quebec Superior Court in a decision th
has aroused deep concern among all Canadians who seek the preservation
civil liberty

The decision is being taken to appeal with the assistance of the Canadian Ci
Liberties Union. Money is urgently needed to carry the appeal through

Clip out this advertisement and send it with your cheque to

The Canadian Civil Liberties Union
1405 Peel Street Montreal, Qu

Charlie Millar's "stork derby" ends with $165,000 payments to four mothers of nine.

Strange Contest Approaches Climax

Seven Toronto Women Hope to Win Millar's $500,000.

10-YEAR STORK DERBY

Mining disaster and rescue at Moose River, N.S., attracts international attention.

EXTRA CLIMAX NEARS IN RACE WITH DEATH

THE HALIFAX HERALD

WHERE RESCUE MEN STAGE NEW RACE AGAINST DEATH

One Is Dead!

Fate Of Two Others Hangs In Balance

Rescuers Start New Race With Death

Hardships Are Suffered By Rescue Men

Greatest News We've Ever Had, Children Say

Thankfulness Of Canada Extended

An Epic Of Fortitude Courage And Devotion

ward VIII abdicates throne
ved divorcee Wallis Simpson.

THE TORONTO DAILY STAR

ORLD WAITS TO HEAR EX-KING'S FAREWELL

HOME AND SPORT EDITION

RD'S REIGN ENDS
E GIVES ASSENT
ABDICATION BILL

EDWARD WEEPS SAYING GOOD-BY TO HIS BROTHER

REBEL LEADER'S LEAFLET BARRAGE FALLS ON MADRID

CHRISTMAS MONARCH CHALLENGING HEARTS IN DRIVE FOR FUNDS

EX-MONARCH MAY BEGIN VOLUNTARY EXILE TO-NIGHT

ALIEN TROOPS ENTER SPAIN AT "MOST ALARMING RATE"

MRS. SIMPSON SURROUNDED BY EXTRA FRENCH POLICE

LEAVES COURT WHEN NAME MISPRONOUNCED

:.N. Pogue's revolutionary
arburetor invention is
tolen from Winnipeg shop.

1937

Iockey star Howie Morenz dies
of injuries sustained in game.

The Governor General's Awards for literature are established.

Trans-Canada Airlines begins service as public corporation.

General Motors workers stage strike in Oshawa, Ont.

CANADIAN NATIONAL TELEGRAM

STANDARD TIME

TORONTO ONT 136P APR 11-37

MR H THOMPSON

UNION HEADQUARTERS UNITED AUTO WORKERS INTERNATIONAL UNION

TORONTO MAY DAY CONFERENCE WITH ONE HUNDRED AND FIFTY TRADE UNIONS AND OTHER LABOR ORGANIZATIONS ASSEMBLED AT MEETING LABOR TEMPLE TORONTO UNANIMOUSLY ADOPTED RESOLUTION OF GREETINGS AND EXPRESSIONS OF SOLIDARITY TO YOU GENERAL MOTOR STRIKERS STOP ON BEHALF OF TENS OF THOUSANDS OF MEMBERS OUR AFFILIATED ORGANIZATIONS [illegible] PLEDGE TO YOU OUR WHOLEHEARTED MORAL AND FINANCIAL SUPPORT UNTIL [illegible] HISTORIC STRIKE IS WON.

TORONTO MAY DAY CONFERENCE, REV BEN H [illegible]

Yellowknife, N.W.T., is founded

The Rowell Commission is set up to study federal-provincial relations.

Imperial Airways' flying boat arrives in Montreal–a new approach to air travel.

Morley Callaghan publishes *More Joy In Heaven.*

1938

Unemployed stage sit-down strike at Vancouver's Central Post Office.

The ballpoint pen comes into common use.

Bluenose wins International Fisherman's Trophy race against American *Thébaud.*

Niagara's 1,400 foot Honeymoon Bridge collapses.

Edmonton Journal is first newspaper outside U.S. to win Pulitzer Prize.

1939

TCA inaugurates first passenger flight Vancouver to Montreal.

Nylon stockings make their appearance.

Saskatchewan's Dorothy Walton wins All-England Badminton Championships.

First automatic starting gate introduced at Whittier Park Race Track, St. Boniface, Man.

King George VI [illegible]
Elizabeth first r[illegible]
monarchs to tour Canada.

Dr. Norman Bethune dies while serving in North China.

Britain declares war on Germany; and one week later Canada declares war.